New South Wales Mathematics Syllabus

New Syllabus MENTALS and Extension

Paul Nightingale

EARLY STAGE ONE

A
FIVE SENSES
PUBLICATION

A FIVE SENSES PUBLICATION

Copyright © 2022 Paul Nightingale - Five Senses Education Pty. Ltd.
New Syllabus Mentals and Extension - Early Stage One Kindergarten

Published by:
Five Senses Education Pty Ltd.
ABN: 16 001 414 437
2/195 Prospect Highway Seven Hills NSW 2147
Ph: 02 9838 9265
email: sevenhills@fivesenseseducation.com.au
website: www.fivesenseseducation.com.au

Cover Design: Brooke Lewis

National Library of Australia Card No.
and ISBN 978-1-76032-401-8

About this Book for the Teacher

New South Wales Mathematics K-2 Syllabus has been developed to help raise the standard of mathematics in the first three years of formal schooling. This book, *New Syllabus Maths, Early Stage One Kindergarten - Mentals and Extension* reinforces and extends the activities introduced in *New Syllabus Maths, Early Stage One Kindergarten*. Work in this book can also be used for homework but its main focus is on extension of the foundation introduced in the new syllabus.

Content and suggested activities are an extension of the syllabus guidelines and topics introduced and addressed in *New Syllabus Maths, Early Stage One Kindergarten*. Topic headings treat and develop content under these guidelines which include Number and Algebra, Measurement and Space as well as Statistics and Data.

Some additional topics have been added as Optional Extension to the Syllabus. These include Money, Angles, Lines, Open Shapes and Chance.

While the teacher can select topics and content from any page in this book, it is suggested mental and extension activity topics should follow on from topic content addressed in *New Syllabus and Maths, Early Stage One Kindergarten*.

New Syllabus and Extension, Early Stage One Kindergarten supports *New Syllabus Maths, Early Stage One Kindergarten* book with additional activities and a variety of extensions and further exposure to concepts and knowledge needed to be successful in Maths.

A full set of answers is provided at the back of the book to assist students, teachers and parents.

Message to Parents

School introduces the child to knowledge, skills and learning experiences needed to be successful in the classroom and at school. However, it is the parents who nurture a child from birth establishing values, attitudes and encouragement for the child to be a good family member and a good citizen.

It is when the teacher and parent work together to reinforce the proficiencies, experience and knowledge learned at school, with the attitudes and values of the home, that a child will achieve outstanding results. The encouragement of parents and teachers together set a positive tone for the child's learning environment and progress.

As a parent you help your child learn every day. This book can assist with the learning processes needed for development of mathematics.

Enjoy the journey!

Number 1 - One

Number and Algebra

1. Trace over this numeral.

2. Draw **one red** pencil.

3. Trace over the name for one.

one one

4. Tick the groups of 1, then draw a line from 1 to groups of one.

5. Write how many cupcakes.

Number 2 - Two

Number and Algebra

6. Trace over the numeral 2.

2222

7. Draw a group with **two** in it.

8. Trace over the name for **two**.

two two

9. Tick the groups of 2.
Draw a line from 2 to groups of 2.

10. Count the balloons then write how many.

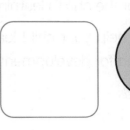

Number and Algebra

1. Trace over the numeral **3**.

2. Draw three groups of three.

3. Trace over the name for **3**.

4. Colour the group with 3 in it.

5. How many apples?

6. Match the numbers to their names.

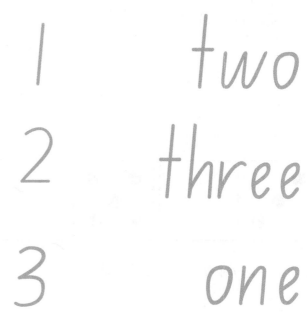

7. Count the fruit then write the total.

a. and make

b. and make

c. and make

8. How many left when two are crossed off?

leaves

9. Fill in the missing number.

Number and Algebra

1. Trace over the numeral 4.

2. Draw 4 dots on each domino.

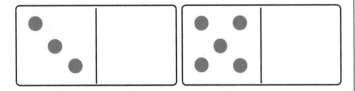

3. Trace over the name for **4**.

4. Colour the groups of **4**.

5. Count the balls then write the totals.

a.

b.

6. Count how many in each group, then write the total.

a.  and ... make [ ]

b.  and ... make [ ]

c.  and ... make [ ]

7. Draw a line from each number to its name as a word.

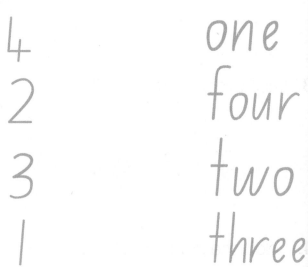

4   one
2   four
3   two
1   three

8. How many left when two crossed off?

4 take away 2 leaves [ ]

9. Fill in the missing number.

4 take away 3 leaves [ ]

Number and Algebra

1. Trace over the numeral 5.

5 5 5 5 5

2. Draw 4 groups of five.

3. Trace over the name for **5**.

five   five

4. Fill in the missing numbers.

1 ___ 3 ___ ___

5. Count the balloons then write how many.

6. Count the number in each group. Write the numeral.

a.  _____

b.  _____

c.  _____

7. Fill in the **missing** numbers counting backwards.

5 ___ 3 ___ ___

8. Draw **three** dots on each domino.

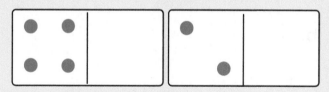

9. Fill in the missing numbers.

a. **2** and **3** make

b. **4** and **1** make

10. Write each number as a numeral.

four

two

Number 6 – six

Number and Algebra

1. Trace over the numeral 6.

2. Draw **6** marbles in each group.

3. Count the stars in each group then write the total as a number.

a.  _____

b.  _____

c.  _____

d.  _____

4. Trace over the name for **6**.

six   six

5. Fill in the missing numbers.

a.

b.

Number 6 Extensions

6. Colour the group with **six** in it.

7. Count how many in each group, then write the total.

a.

b.

8. Write the total number of dots below each domino.

9. Fill in the missing numbers.

1 ___ 3 4 ___ ___

10. How many more are needed to make **6**?

Number 7 - seven

Number and Algebra

1. Trace over each copy of the word **seven** and number **7**.

seven   7

seven   7

2. Colour **7** balloons.

3. Fill in the missing numbers.

3 _____ _____ 6 _____

4. Fill in the missing numbers to make **7**.

a. **5** and ☐ make **7**

b. **2** and ☐ make **7**

c. ☐ and **4** make **7**

5. Write next counting number.

a. **5,** ☐   b. **6,** ☐

Number 7 Extensions

6. Count the number of dots then write how many below each domino.

☐   ☐   ☐

7. How many are left when some are crossed off?

a.  leaves ☐

b.  leaves ☐

8. Fill in the missing number.

a. **4** take away **2** leaves ☐

b. **7** take away ☐ leaves **3**

9. How many fish in each bowl?

a.    b.

☐   ☐

10. Fill in the missing numbers counting backward from **7**.

7 ___ ___ **4** ___ **2** ___

Number and Algebra

1. Trace over the numeral 8.

8 8 8 8

2. Draw **8** circles. Colour them differently.

3. Colour the groups with **8** stars.

a.

b.

c.

4. Write the numbers **before** and **after** these.

a. ___ 6 ___   b. ___ 4 ___

c. ___ 7 ___   d. ___ 5 ___

5. Trace over **8** written as words.

eight eight

6. Count the dots on the dominoes then add them and write the total.

a. and make ⬜

b. and make ⬜

c. and make ⬜

7. Write how many in each group below the fish bowls, then add the total.

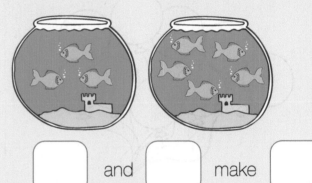

⬜ and ⬜ make ⬜

8. Count the tennis balls then cross off **4** and write how many left.

 leaves ⬜

9. Fill in the missing number for each of these

a. 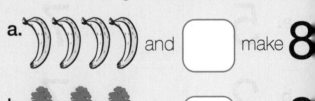 and ⬜ make **8**

b. and ⬜ make **8**

10. Fill in the missing numbers.

a. **3** and **5** make ⬜

b. **8** take away ⬜ leaves **6**

Number 9 – nine

Number and Algebra

1. Trace over the numeral **9**.

2. Draw nine squares.

3. Draw dots on the dominoes so they all make **9**.

a.

b.

c.

d.

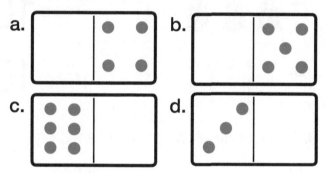

4. Fill in the missing counting numbers.

_____ 6 _____ 8 _____

5. Trace over the name for **9**.

nine   nine

6. Count the eggs in each carton, then write the total number of eggs.

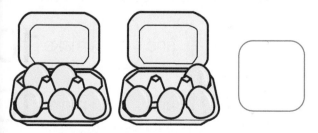

Number 9 Extensions

7. Write the missing number in each combination to **9**.

a. **1** and ☐ make **9**

b. **2** and ☐ make **9**

c. **3** and ☐ make **9**

d. **4** and ☐ make **9**

e. **5** and ☐ make **9**

8. How many left when some are crossed off?

a.  ☐

b. 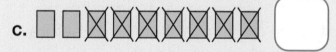 ☐

c. ☐

9. Fill in the missing numbers.

a. ☐ take away **3** leaves **6**

b. **9** take away ☐ leaves **5**

10. How many more needed to make **9**?

a. ✳✳✳✳ and ☐ make **9**

b. ⬆⬆⬆ and ☐ make **9**

c. ♥♥♥♥♥ and ☐ make **9**

Number 10 – ten

Number and Algebra

1. Trace over the number **10**.

10 10 10 10

2. Colour the group with **ten** counters.

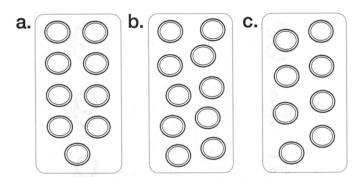

a.　　　b.　　　c.

3. Draw a group of **ten** triangles.

4. Write the number that comes **before** each of these numbers.

a. ___ 7　b. ___ 3　c. ___ 6

5. Add dots to each domino to make **10**.

a.　　　b.

c.

6. Trace over the name for **10**.

ten ten ten

Number 10 Extensions

7. Write the missing number in each combination to **ten**.

a. **1** and **9** make ▢

b. ▢ and **8** make **10**

c. **3** and ▢ make **10**

d. **4** and ▢ make **10**

e. ▢ and **5** make **10**

8. How many more needed to make **10**?

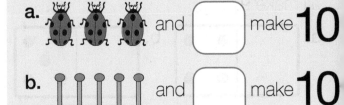

a. 🐞🐞🐞 and ▢ make **10**

b. ❘❘❘❘❘ and ▢ make **10**

9. How many left when some are crossed of

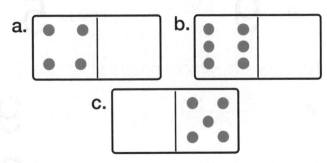

a. ✓✓✓✓✓✓✓✗✗ ▢

b. ❘❘❘✗✗✗✗✗✗✗ ▢

10. Fill in the missing numbers.

a. **10** take away **6** leaves ▢

b. **10** take away **3** leaves ▢

11. How many more needed to make **10**

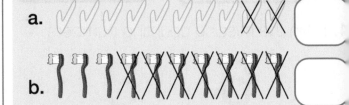

a. ⬆⬆⬆⬆⬆⬆ and ▢ make **10**

b. ╱╱╱╱╱╱╱╱╱ and ▢ make **10**

1. Zero means the same as nought, nothing or none. Trace over zero.

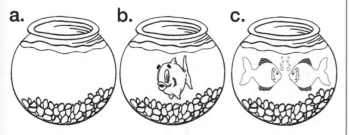

2. Colour the fish bowl with **zero** fish.

a.   b.   c.

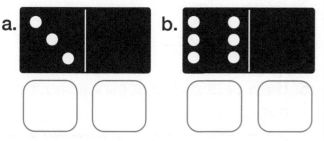

3. Trace over the name **zero**.

zero   zero

4. Fill in the missing numbers. Begin at **0**.

____ 1 ____ 3 4 ____

5. Write the number of dots below each part of a domino.

a.   b.

6. Join the dots to complete the house. Begin at **zero**.

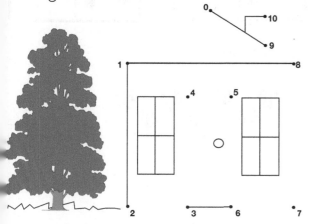

7. Match the correct word to the number of fish in each tank.

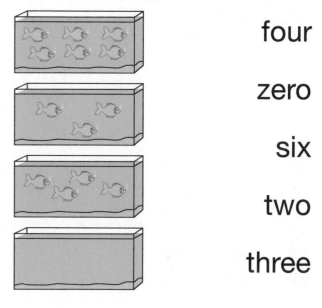

four

zero

six

two

three

8. Write the missing numbers.

a. 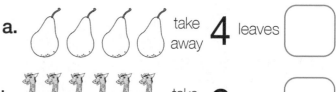 take away **4** leaves ☐

b.  take away **6** leaves ☐

c.  take away **5** leaves ☐

9. Fill in the missing numbers.

a. **8** take away **8** leaves ☐

b. **3** take away **3** leaves ☐

10. Fill in the missing numbers.

a. **8** and ☐ make **8**

b. ☐ and **7** make **7**

c. **9** and ☐ make **9**

Number and Algebra

1. Trace over each **number** in words.
Match each name to the right group.

six

three

zero

five

ten

seven

nine

eight

one

four

two

2. Count back and fill in the missing
numbers.

10 ___ ___ ___

6 ___

Number and Algebra

3. Add the **next** counting numbers to each
group.

a. 4 5 6 ___ ___

b. 3 4 5 ___ ___

c. 6 7 8 ___ ___

4. Write the missing numbers in each group

a. 2 3 ___ ___ 5 ___

b. 4 ___ ___ 6 7 ___

c. 5 6 ___ ___ ___ 9

5. Draw dots on the dominoes so they all
make 9.

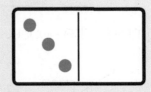 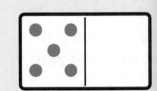

6. How many in each group?

a. ♥ ♥ ♥ ♥ ♥ ___

b. ○○○○○○○○○ ___

New Syllabus Mentals and Extension K, Early Stage On

Number and Algebra

1. Draw a line from the ordinal number to its name.

1st   fifth

5th   tenth

7th   first

10th   seventh

2. Colour the **1st** car blue and the **4th** car red.

3. Fill in the missing ordinal numbers.

1st			4th	5th	

4. Colour the rosette for **first** place blue, **second** place red and **third** place yellow.

5. Draw a **4th**, **5th** and **6th** block on the stack.

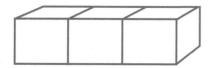

6. Write the fourth letter of the alphabet.

7. What position is letter H in the alphabet?

8. Number the runners first to last as an ordinal number.

9. Match the ordinal number to its name.

first   6th

third   1st

sixth   2nd

second   3rd

10. Write the ordinal number **before** and **after** each of these.

a. _____ 2nd _____

b. _____ 8th _____

c. _____ 6th _____

11. What is the seventh letter of the alphabet?

Numbers 11, 12 and 13

1. Trace over each number and their names.

a. *11 eleven*

b. *12 twelve*

c. *13 thirteen*

2. Colour the group with 12 balls.

a.

b.

3. Write the numbers **before** and **after** these.

a. ___ 11 ___   b. ___ 10 ___

c. ___ 12 ___   d. ___ 9 ___

4. Fill in the missing numbers.

a.

9	10			

b.

13	12			

5. Count how many in each group then write totals.

a.  and ☆☆ make ☐

b. 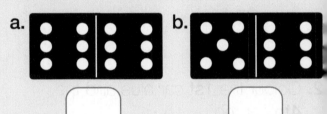 and 🍎🍎 make ☐

6. Count the dots then write how many.

a. ☐   b. ☐

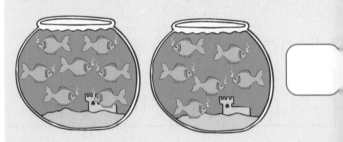

7. How many fish in these two bowls?

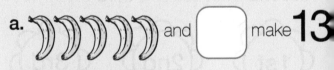 ☐

8. Fill in the missing numbers.

a. 🍌🍌🍌🍌🍌 and ☐ make **13**

b. 🍊🍊🍊🍊🍊🍊 and ☐ make **11**

9. Count the matches and write the totals.

a.   b.   c.

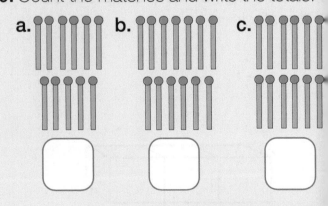

☐   ☐   ☐

1. Trace over the numbers in words then write the numbers.

a. fourteen 14 14

b. fifteen 15 15

c. sixteen 16 16

2. Count the buttons, then write the totals. Colour the group with 14 counters.

a. 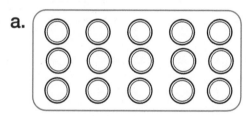 _____

b. 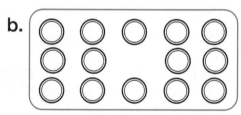 _____

c. 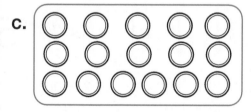 _____

3. Fill in the missing numbers.

a. [ ] and ⬜ make **14**

b. 🍐🍐🍐🍐🍐 and [ ] make **15**

4. Fill in the missing numbers.

11			14	15

5. Fill in the numbers **before** and **after** these.

a. ____ 15 ____   b. ____ 12 ____

c. ____ 14 ____   d. ____ 13 ____

6. Colour 16 balloons.

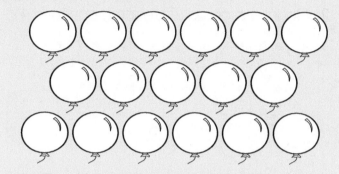

7. Complete these number sentences.

a. $6 + 7 =$ [ ]   b. $8 + 8 =$ [ ]

c. $9 + 5 =$ [ ]   d. $10 + 6 =$ [ ]

8. How many more counters are needed to make 15?

a. ●●●●● ●●●● and [ ] make **15**

b. ●●●●● ●●●●● and [ ] make **15**

9. Fill in the missing numbers.

		14		12	11

10. How many in this group of triangles.

 [ ]

Numbers 17 and 18	Numbers 19 and 20

Numbers 17 and 18

1. Trace over the number and its name in words.

a. 17 17 seventeen

b. 18 18 eighteen

2. Count the group. Colour the one with 17.

a.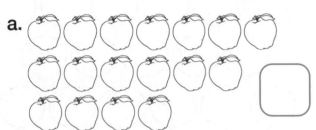

b.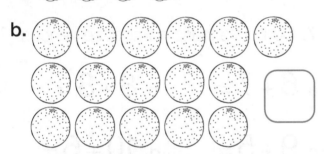

3. Write the numbers **before** and **after** these.

a. ___ 17 ___   b. ___ 18 ___

4. Fill in the missing numbers.

a.
11			14			17

b.
18			15	13	

5. Write the value for these blocks.

a. 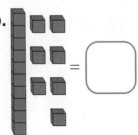 =

b. =

Numbers 19 and 20

6. Trace over these numbers.

19 19 20 20

7. Colour the group with **19** apples.

a.    b.

c.

8. How many more needed to make 20?

a. [llllllll] and [ ] make **20**

b. [↓↓↓↓↓↓↓↓↓↓] and [ ] make **15**

9. How many are left when some are crossed off? Fill in the sentence.

[ ] take away [ ] leaves [ ]

10. Write in counting order.

18	14	19	16	13	17	15

New Syllabus Mentals and Extension K, Early Stage On

1. Write the numbers **before** and **after** these.

a. _____ 7 _____   b. _____ 12 _____

2. Count the dots then write the totals.

 and make ☐

3. Match the number to its name.

eight   twelve   six   zero   fourteen   nine   seventeen   twenty

(9) (0) (8) (20) (12) (6) (14) (17)

4. Count the matches in each group.

a.  _____   b. _____   c. 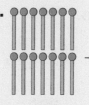 _____   d. _____

5. Fill in the missing numbers on the counting table.

1	2			5
	7	8		
11			14	
	17		19	

6. How many dots need to be added to the dominoes to total 19?

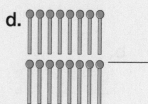 make 19 ☐

7. Fill in the missing numbers.

a. 7 and 8 make ☐

b. 12 and 6 make ☐

3. Write these numbers **backwards** in counting order from 20.

15   19   17   14   18   16

20					

9. How many are left when five are crossed off. Fill in the sentence.

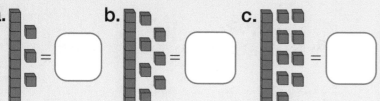

☐ take away 5 leaves ☐

10. Count the blocks and write the totals.

a.  = ☐   b. = ☐   c. = ☐

11. What is the 6th letter of the alphabet? ☐

12. Write the number 20 in words.

_____

Adding Groups and Numbers

1. Use two colours to make 2 equal groups.

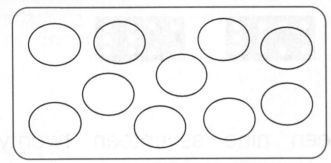

2. Count the groups. Write the numbers.

a.

[ ] and [ ] make **6**

b.

[ ] and [ ] make **6**

c.
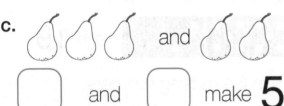

[ ] and [ ] make **5**

3. Draw **three** more shapes.
Add them and write the numeral.

a.  and   make [ ]

b.  and   make [ ]

c.   and   make [ ]

4. Fill in the missing numbers.

a. **4** and **9** make [ ]

b. **5** and **7** make [ ]

c. **9** and **8** make [ ]

Adding Groups

5. Use **3** colours to make **three** groups.

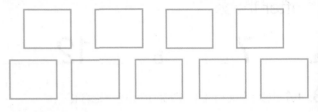

6. Add **three** shapes to make the number sentence.

a.
 and   make [ ]

b.
 and   make [ ]

c.  and   make [ ]

7. Finish this pattern.

8. Add numerals to complete the number sentences.

a. **4** and **2** make [ ]

b. **5** and **2** make [ ]

c. **1** and **4** make [ ]

9. Add these groups together. Write totals.

a.  and   make [ ]

b.  and   make [ ]

New Syllabus Mentals and Extension K, Early Stage On

Adding Numbers	**Adding to Ten**

1. Complete these number sentences.

a. **8** and ⬜ make **9**

b. **3** and **6** make ⬜

c. ⬜ and **2** make **9**

2. Count the number in each group.
Write the numerals in the squares.

a.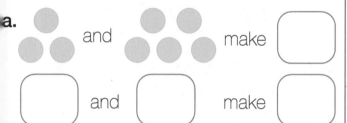

⬜ and ⬜ make ⬜

b.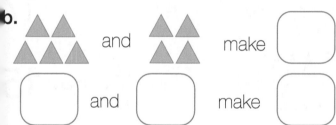

⬜ and ⬜ make ⬜

c.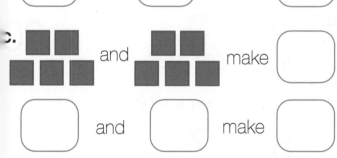

⬜ and ⬜ make ⬜

3. Add the dots on the dominoes.
Fill in the number sentence.

a.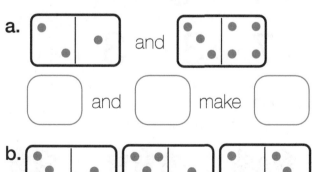

⬜ and ⬜ make ⬜

b.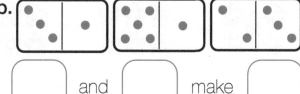

⬜ and ⬜ make ⬜

4. Add the groups of matches.

a. 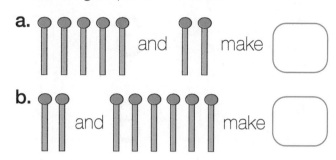 and make ⬜

b.  and make ⬜

5. Complete these number sentences.

a. **4** and ⬜ make **10**

b. ⬜ and **5** make **10**

c. **7** and ⬜ make **10**

6. Add balloons to each group to make 5.
Fill in the number sentence.

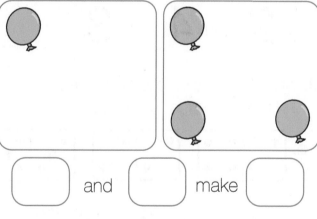

⬜ and ⬜ make ⬜

7. Add the number in a group.
Fill in the number sentence.

a.

⬜ and ⬜ make ⬜

b.

⬜ and ⬜ make ⬜

1. Add these.

a.  and **3** make ☐

b.  and **3** make ☐

c. and **3** make ☐

2. Add these.

a. **6** and **2** and **5** = ☐

b. **5** and **4** and **6** = ☐

c. **2** and **4** and **3** = ☐

3. Add the dots on the dominoes.
Fill in the number sentence.

a.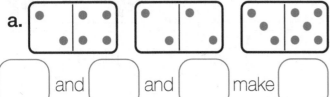

☐ and ☐ and ☐ make ☐

b.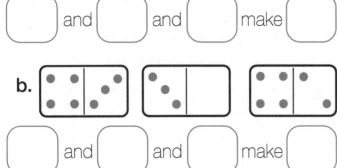

☐ and ☐ and ☐ make ☐

4. Count how many then add 7.

a. 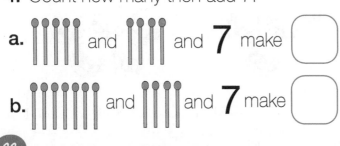 and and **7** make ☐

b. and and **7** make ☐

5. Count the objects. Write the number.
Fill in the number sentence.

a.  and and make ☐

☐ and ☐ and ☐ make ☐

b. and and make ☐

☐ and ☐ and ☐ make ☐

6. Add the group and write a number
to complete the sentence.

a.  and and ☐ make **17**

b.  and ☐ and make **15**

c. and and ☐ make **20**

7. Complete these additions.

a. **5** and **7** make ☐

b. **4** and **9** make ☐

c. **7** and **3** and **3** make ☐

8. Count these items.
Fill in the number sentence.

 and and

☐ and ☐ and ☐ make ☐

New Syllabus Mentals and Extension K, Early Stage On

Number Line Additions

1. Add the numbers along the line.
Write an answer.

a. **7** and **2** make ☐

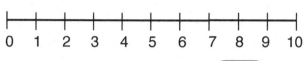

b. **1** and **6** make ☐

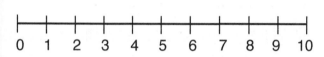

2. Fill in the sentences shown on the number lines.

a.

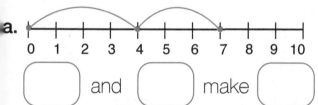

☐ and ☐ make ☐

b.

☐ and ☐ make ☐

c.

☐ and ☐ make ☐

3. Show the sentences and totals on the number lines.

a.

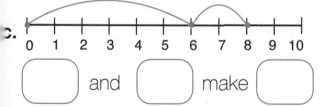

5 and **3** make ☐

b.

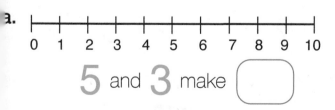

4 and **2** make ☐

Adding Three Numbers

4. Add the numbers on the line.
Fill in the number sentence.

a.

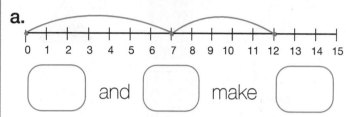

☐ and ☐ make ☐

b.

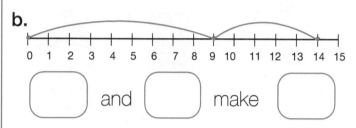

☐ and ☐ make ☐

c.

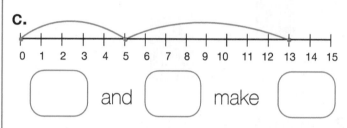

☐ and ☐ make ☐

5. Count the number of jumps along the line. Write the numbers and add them.

a.

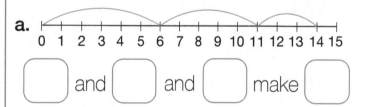

☐ and ☐ and ☐ make ☐

b.

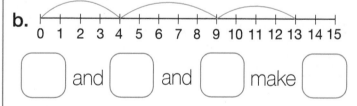

☐ and ☐ and ☐ make ☐

6. Use the number sentence to count along the line. Write an answer.

a. **7** and **2** and **4** make ☐

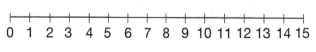

b. **2** and **5** and **6** make ☐

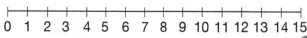

Patterns and Puzzles

1. Finish the patterns.

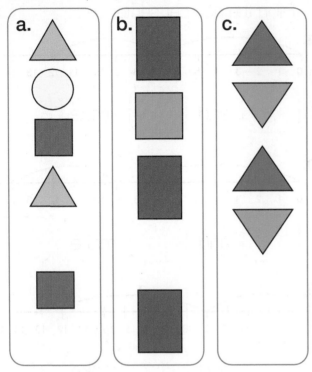

2. Complete the tile pattern.

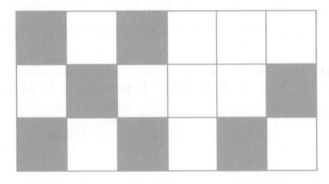

3. Complete the pattern across the page.

4. Draw a line to the shapes that might fit together.

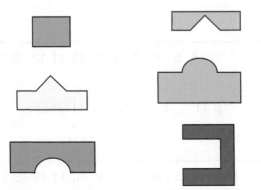

More Patterns and Puzzles

5. Complete this pattern.

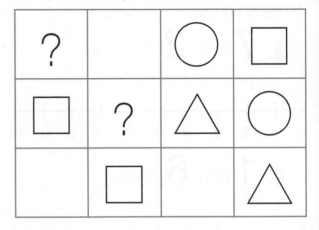

6. Fill in the missing shapes in the pattern.

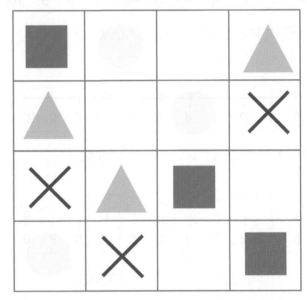

7. Add the missing symbols to finish the pattern.

O	?	X	+	O
+	O			+
X			?	X
?		+	O	?

8. Continue the pattern of coloured shapes.

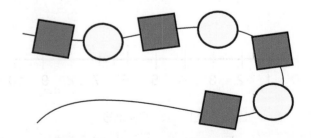

     New Syllabus Mentals and Extension K, Early Stage On

1. Write the numbers for this group.

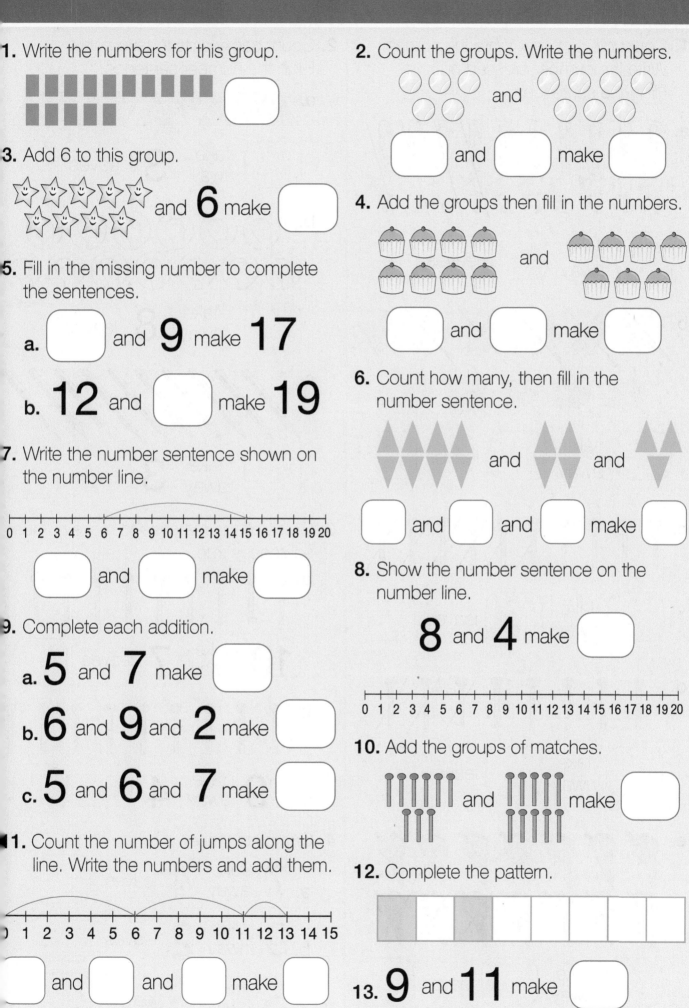

2. Count the groups. Write the numbers.

◯◯◯ ◯◯ and ◯◯◯◯ ◯◯◯

☐ and ☐ make ☐

3. Add 6 to this group.

and **6** make ☐

4. Add the groups then fill in the numbers.

and

☐ and ☐ make ☐

5. Fill in the missing number to complete the sentences.

a. ☐ and **9** make **17**

b. **12** and ☐ make **19**

6. Count how many, then fill in the number sentence.

and and

☐ and ☐ and ☐ make ☐

7. Write the number sentence shown on the number line.

0 1 2 3 4 5 6 7 8 9 10 11 12 13 14 15 16 17 18 19 20

☐ and ☐ make ☐

8. Show the number sentence on the number line.

8 and **4** make ☐

0 1 2 3 4 5 6 7 8 9 10 11 12 13 14 15 16 17 18 19 20

9. Complete each addition.

a. **5** and **7** make ☐

b. **6** and **9** and **2** make ☐

c. **5** and **6** and **7** make ☐

10. Add the groups of matches.

and make ☐

11. Count the number of jumps along the line. Write the numbers and add them.

0 1 2 3 4 5 6 7 8 9 10 11 12 13 14 15

☐ and ☐ and ☐ make ☐

12. Complete the pattern.

13. **9** and **11** make ☐

Subtraction and Cross Off Method

1. Count the pictures. Write the number.
Write the number crossed out.
Fill in the sentence.

a.

◯ take away ◯ leaves ◯

b.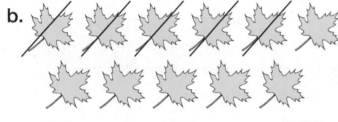

◯ take away ◯ leaves ◯

c.

◯ take away ◯ leaves ◯

d.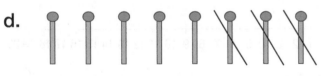

◯ take away ◯ leaves ◯

e.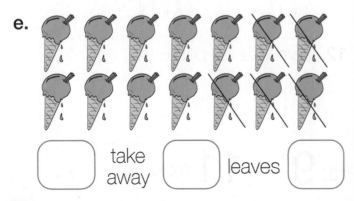

◯ take away ◯ leaves ◯

Subtraction – Counting Backwards

2. Count backwards to take away.
Fill in the number sentence.

a.
◯ take away **3** leaves ◯

b.
◯ take away **8** leaves ◯

c.
◯ take away **3** leaves ◯

3. Cross off the matches to make number sentences true.

a.
10 take away **7** leaves ◯

b.
9 take away **4** leaves ◯

4. Complete these.

a. **7** take away **4** leaves ◯

b. **9** take away **2** leaves ◯

c. **5** take away **3** leaves ◯

New Syllabus Mentals and Extension K, Early Stage One

Subtraction

1. Count the oranges, write the number in the first box. Cross off 4 oranges. Fill in the number sentence.

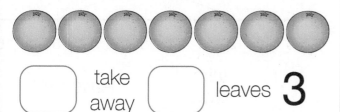

◯ take away ◯ leaves **3**

2. Count the stars, write the number in the first box. Cross some off until 5 are left. Fill in the sentence.

◯ take away ◯ leaves **5**

3. Count the objects in each group, then take away 4 and 6.

a.  take away **4** leaves ◯

b.  take away **6** leaves ◯

4. Try these. Complete the sentences.

a. **8** take away **3** leaves ◯

b. **7** take away **1** leaves ◯

c. **10** take away **5** leaves ◯

d. **9** take away **7** leaves ◯

Subtraction - Less Than

5. Complete these sentences.

a. **4** less than **10** is ◯

b. **6** less than **14** is ◯

c. **7** less than **15** is ◯

d. **12** less than **18** is ◯

6. Count the dots then complete the take away sentences.

a.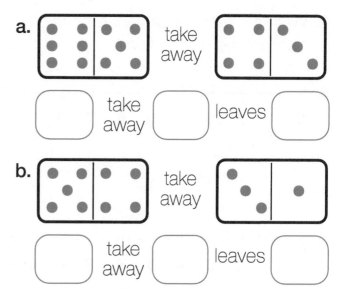

◯ take away ◯ leaves ◯

b.

◯ take away ◯ leaves ◯

7. Count the balloons. Cross off 9 then complete the sentence to match.

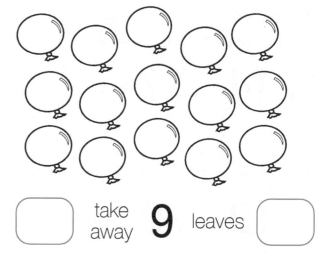

◯ take away **9** leaves ◯

8. **20** take away **17** leaves ◯

Subtraction on a Number Line

1. Start with the first number and count **backwards** on the line. Write an answer.

a. 9 take away 7 leaves ☐

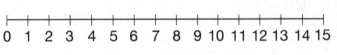
`0 1 2 3 4 5 6 7 8 9 10 11 12 13 14 15`

b. 12 take away 7 leaves ☐

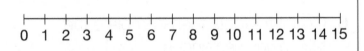
`0 1 2 3 4 5 6 7 8 9 10 11 12 13 14 15`

2. Write the number sentence for these number line subtractions.

a.
`0 1 2 3 4 5 6 7 8 9 10`

☐ take away ☐ leaves ☐

b.
`0 1 2 3 4 5 6 7 8 9 10`

☐ take away ☐ leaves ☐

3. Start with the first number and count **backwards** on the line. Write an answer.

a. 14 take away 7 leaves ☐

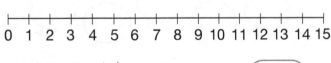
`0 1 2 3 4 5 6 7 8 9 10 11 12 13 14 15`

b. 12 take away 9 leaves ☐

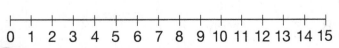
`0 1 2 3 4 5 6 7 8 9 10 11 12 13 14 15`

Number Line Subtraction

4. Count backwards on the number line to take away. Write the numbers in the sentences.

a.
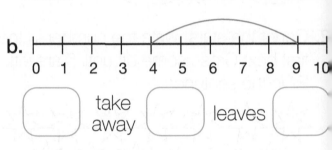
`0 1 2 3 4 5 6 7 8 9 10`

☐ take away ☐ leaves ☐

b.
`0 1 2 3 4 5 6 7 8 9 10`

☐ take away ☐ leaves ☐

5. Show these sentences on the number line.

a. 10 take away 2 leaves 8

`0 1 2 3 4 5 6 7 8 9 10`

b. 7 take away 4 leaves 3

`0 1 2 3 4 5 6 7 8 9 10`

c. 9 take away 7 leaves 2

`0 1 2 3 4 5 6 7 8 9 10`

6. Complete these.

a. 2 less than 6 is ☐

b. 4 less than 9 is ☐

c. 9 less than 15 is ☐

New Syllabus Mentals and Extension K, Early Stage On

1. Draw a line to join the circles that are the same size. Colour each group.

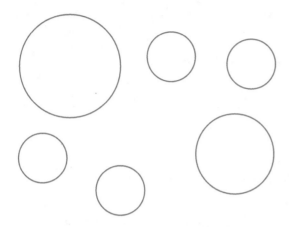

2. Draw in each missing shape.

a.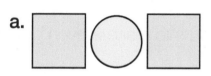

b.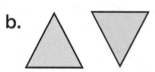

c.

3. Colour the one that **doesn't** belong in this group.

4. Colour the one that **does NOT** belong.

5. Draw a line from each object to the group it fits best.

6. Add these shapes to complete the pattern.

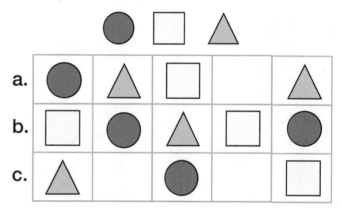

7. Colour the one that is **different** in each pattern.

a.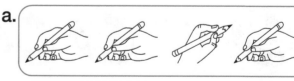

b.

c.

Sorting Groups

1. Colour everything that has **4 legs**.

2. Colour the objects that grow on trees.

3. Colour the one that does **NOT** belong.

4. Tick the ones that can fly.

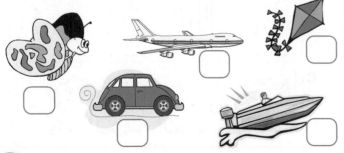

Organising Groups

5. Write the number in each group.

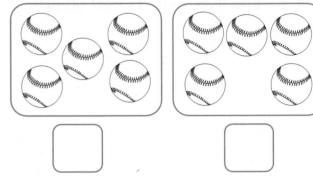

6. Fill in the number sentence.

7. Use two colours to make 2 even groups of stars.

8. Fill in the number sentence.

9. Count how many in each group then complete sentences.

a.

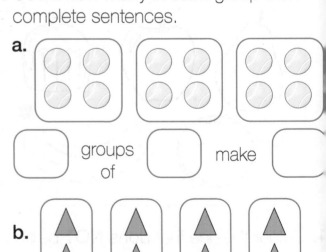

b.

New Syllabus Mentals and Extension K, Early Stage On

Make Equal Groups

1. Use 3 coloured pencils to make **three equal** parts.

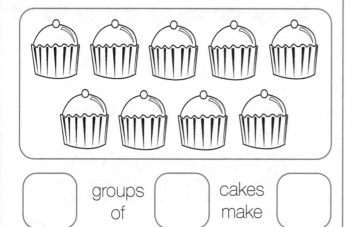

| groups of | cakes make | |

2. Use two coloured pencils to make **2 equal** groups of **5 counters**.

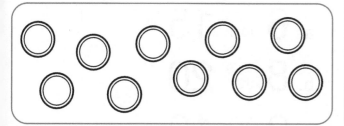

3. Show the groups of counters as a number sentence.

| groups of | counters make | |

4. Add fish to the right hand bowl to make **2 equal groups**.

5. Colour the counters to make **4 equal groups** of 4.

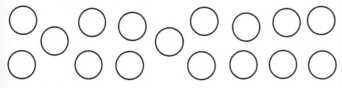

Making Groups

6. Draw extra objects to match the number sentences.

a.

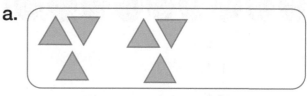

3 groups of **3**

b.

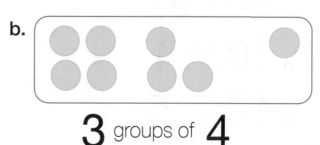

3 groups of **4**

7. Write the number sentences for these equal groups.

a.

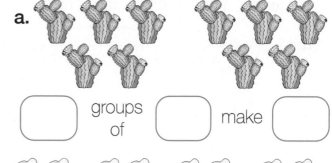

| groups of | make | |

b.

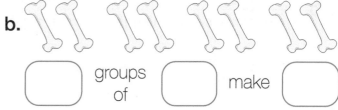

| groups of | make | |

8. Make 4 groups of 2 counters.

9. Complete this sentence about apples.

| groups of | make | |

1. Complete the sentence for the apples.

[ ] take away [ ] leaves [ ]

2. Count backwards to take away. Complete the number sentence.

[ ] take away **5** leaves [ ]

3. Complete these sentences.

a. **9** take away **6** leaves [ ]

b. **10** take away **4** leaves [ ]

c. **12** take away **5** leaves [ ]

d. **20** take away **11** leaves [ ]

4. Cross off 7 counters. Fill in the number sentence.

[ ] take away [ ] leaves **8**

5. Complete these sentences.

a. **6** less than **15** is [ ]

b. **8** less than **20** is [ ]

c. **9** less than **12** is [ ]

d. **11** less than **19** is [ ]

6. Fill in the number sentences for these subtractions shown on the number lines.

a. 0 1 2 3 4 5 6 7 8 9 10 11 12 13 14 15 16 17 18 19 20

[ ] take away [ ] leaves [ ]

b. 0 1 2 3 4 5 6 7 8 9 10 11 12 13 14 15 16 17 18 19 20

[ ] take away [ ] leaves [ ]

7. Draw the missing shape.

☐ △ ○ ___ △ ○

8. Fill in the missing number.

7, 12, 17, [ ], 27, 32

9. Circle the one that does NOT belong to this group.

10. Fill in the number sentences.

a.

[ ] groups of [ ] make [ ]

b.

[ ] groups of [ ] make [ ]

11. Write the number sentence.

[ ] groups of [ ] make [ ]

12. Colour the blocks the make 2 equal groups.

New Syllabus Mentals and Extension K, Early Stage On

1. Draw a line to match each coin value to its face.

2. Draw a line from the coin to its name.

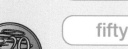

| twenty cents |
| one dollar |
| fifty cents |
| five cents |
| two dollars |
| ten cents |

3. Tick the number of kangaroos on some $1 coins?

4	6	3	5
◯	◯	◯	◯

4. Tick the coin that has lyrebird on its face?

10 cents	20 cents	5 cents	50 cents
◯	◯	◯	◯

5. Order the coins from lowest value to highest value.

☐ ☐ ☐ ☐ ☐ ☐

6. Write each total amount.

a.

0

b.

0

7. Match coins to what they can buy.

 50c

20c

 $2

1. Add the value of these coins

2. Colour the coins needed to buy the icy pole.

3. Add the coins and write the totals.

a.

b.

c.

4. Colour the coins needed to buy these items.

a.

b.

c.

5. Draw a line to match notes to their names.

a.    twenty dollars

b.    ten dollars

c.    five dollars

d.    fifty dollars

e.    one hundred dollars

6. Write these notes using numbers.

a. fifty dollars $

b. twenty dollars $

c. ten dollars $

d. five dollars $

e. one hundred dollars $

7. Write the value of Australian notes lowest to highest.

$ $ $ $ $

8. Which Australian note has the head of the King on one side? $

9. How many $5 notes are needed to equal $20?

1. Write the name of the note in words.

_____

_____

2. Match the notes to what they can buy.

a.

b.

c.

$5

$100

$50

3. Match the coins to what they can buy.

50c $2   50c EACH

4. Add the notes and coins.

a.

= ☐

b.

= ☐

5. Write the colours for these notes.

a. ten dollars _____

b. twenty dollars _____

c. one hundred dollars _____

6. Colour the coins to show these values.

a.  $1.20

b.  $2.55

c.  $1.00

7. Colour the Tap 'n' Go card.

debit

6133 6 00 0000 0000

Valid Thru 00/00

Abby Smith

Happy Birthday

Merry Christmas

A ♥ A

8. Colour the items an adult can buy with a Tap 'n' Go card.

BREAD

9. How many ten dollars notes are needed to equal fifty dollars? ☐

10. Write the total of these coins and notes.

$ ☐

1. Draw a line to match the two halves.

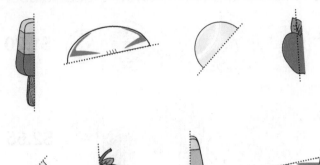

2. Colour half of each object or shape.

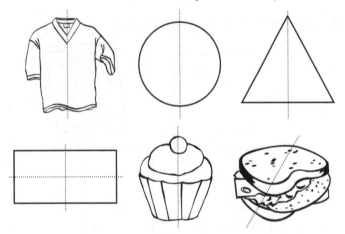

3. Draw a line down the centre of each shape to make two equal halves.

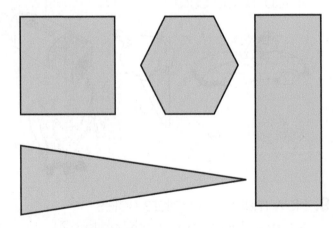

4. Tick the object that shows half.

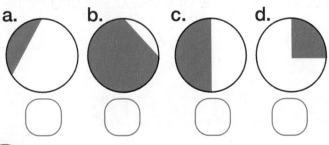

5. Draw a line to match each half to its whole.

a.

b.

c.

d.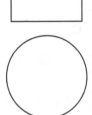

6. Colour half of each group.

a.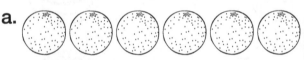

b.

c.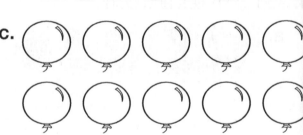

7. Write the number.

a. $\frac{1}{2}$ of 12 = ☐   b. $\frac{1}{2}$ of 8 = ☐

c. $\frac{1}{2}$ of 20 = ☐   d. $\frac{1}{2}$ of 10 = ☐

8. How many half apples in six apples. ☐ half apples

Fractions – Quarter

1. Colour a quarter of each shape.

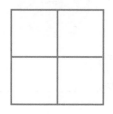  
 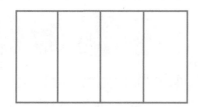

2. Colour the objects that are often cut into quarters or more.

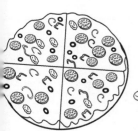 
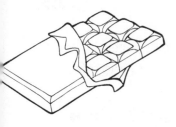 

3. Match each quarter to its whole.

a.   **b.**   **c.**

4. Divide this shape into equal quarters.

Fractions – Quarter Shapes and Groups

5. Colour the shape that can NOT be divided into equal quarters.

6. Colour a quarter of each group.

a.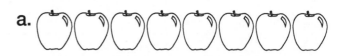

b.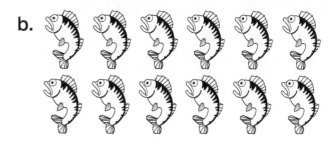

c.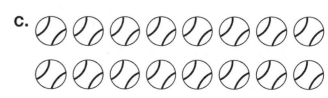

7. Match half or quarter to the shapes.

a.   half **b.**

c.   quarter **d.**

e.   **g.**   **f.**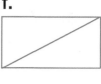

8. Write the number.

a. $\frac{1}{4}$ of 20 = ☐   **b.** $\frac{1}{2}$ of 50 = ☐

c. $\frac{1}{2}$ of 18 = ☐   **d.** $\frac{1}{4}$ of 8 = ☐

1. Draw a line from each line to its name.

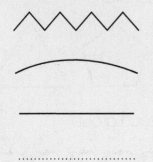

| dotted |
| zig zag |
| curved |
| straight |

2. Tick the lines that do NOT join.

a.   b.   c.

d.   e.   f.

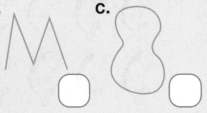

3. Add lines to make closed shapes.

a.   b.   c.   d.

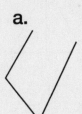  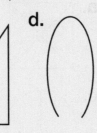

4. Use a zig zag line to finish each line.

a.   b.   c.

  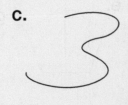

5. Draw an open and closed shape.

OPEN   CLOSED

---

1. Name this coin in words.

_____

2. Which coin has Australia's coat of arms on one side. _____

3. Add these coins.

      $ [ ]

4. What colour are these notes?

a.    b.

_____   _____

5. Colour the coins need to buy the orange

6. How many $10 notes are equal to one hundred dollars? [ ]

7. Is this Tap 'n' Go card?

Yes [ ]   No [ ]

8. What part of the triangle is coloured? Colour the fraction.

 $\frac{1}{2}$ or $\frac{1}{4}$

9. Colour a quarter of this shape.

10. How many in a half of this group?

 [ ]

11. How many in a quarter of this group?

 [ ]

New Syllabus Mentals and Extension K, Early Stage On

1. Colour the **longer** snake.

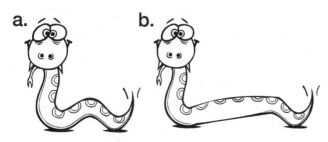

a.   b.

2. Colour the ribbons that are the **same** length.

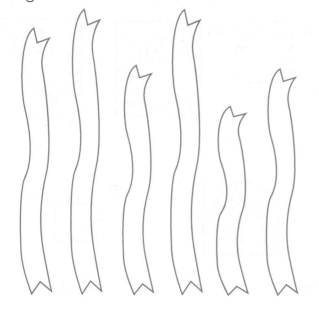

3. Draw a **shorter** pencil.

4. Colour the **long** one in each pair.

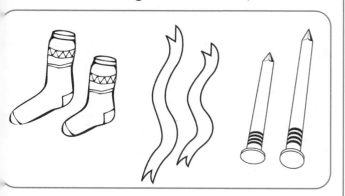

5. Colour the **short** log.

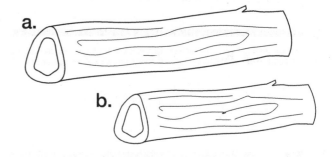

a.

b.

6. Colour the **tallest** tree.

7. Colour the **shortest** pants.

8. Tick the objects **longer** than a peg.

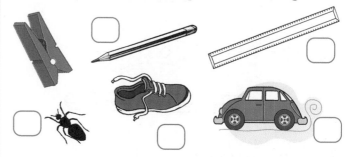

9. Colour the **longest** pencil.

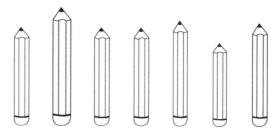

1. Write how many units are shown to measure the length of each line.

a.

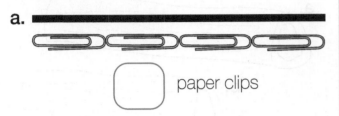

[ ] paper clips

b.

[ ] pencils

c.

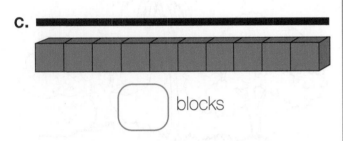

[ ] blocks

d.

[ ] five cent coins

2. Colour the **shortest** object.

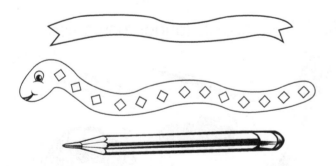

3. Draw a log **longer** than this one, then colour half of it.

4. Colour the shape with the **largest** area.

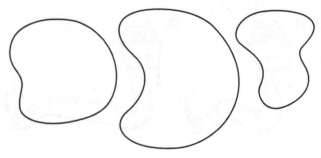

5. Order these squares 1 to 5 from **smallest** to **largest** area.

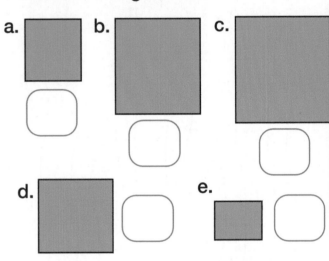

a. [ ]   **b.** [ ]   **c.** [ ]

d. [ ]   **e.** [ ]

6. Colour the objects with the **bigger** area.

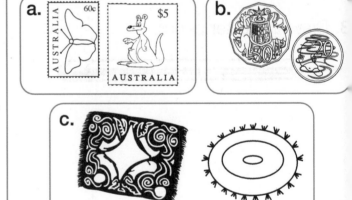

a.   **b.**

c.

7. Count and record the number of squares in each area. Colour the smaller area.

a. **b.**

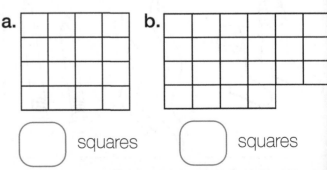

[ ] squares   [ ] squares

1. Colour the shape with the **largest** area.

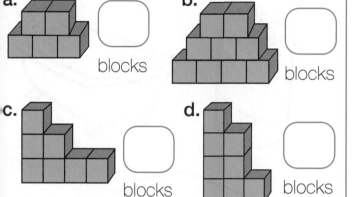

a. ___ blocks

b. ___ blocks

c. ___ blocks

d. ___ blocks

2. Circle the object that takes up the **most** space. (It has the bigger volume.)

a.

b.
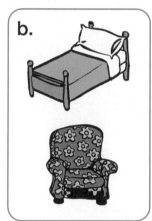

3. Order the volume of blocks 1 to 4, **smallest** to **largest**.

a.
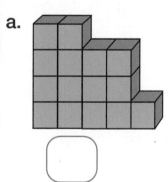

b.
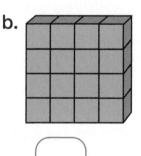

c.
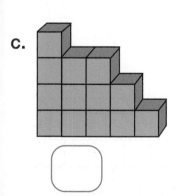

d.
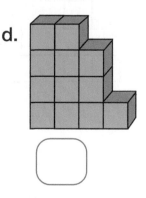

4. Colour the glass **half-full**.

a.   b.   c.

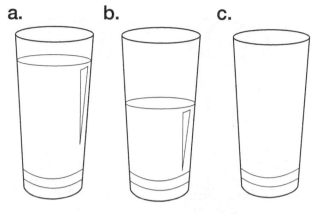

5. Draw a line from the word 'full' to the full bowl.

full

6. Colour the **empty** bottle.

a.   b.   c.

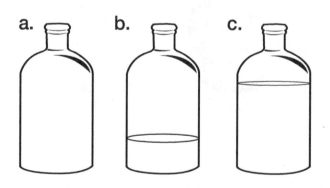

7. Colour the glass that would hold the **most**.

a.

b.   c.
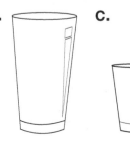

1. Colour the one that might hold the **most**.

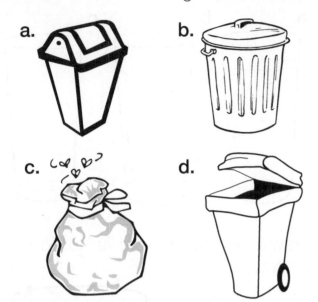

a.   b.

c.   d.

2. Order the objects from 1 to 5 to show holds most to holds least.

3. Colour each glass to where each would be **half full**.

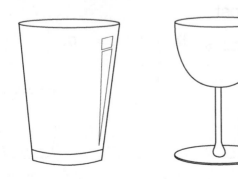

4. Colour the one that holds **least**.

5. Match the words to the capacity of each container.

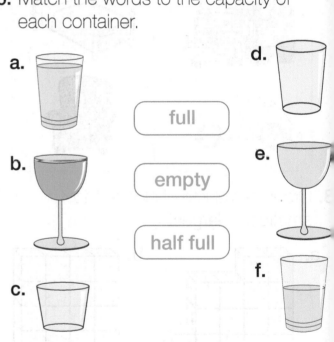

a.   d.

full

b.   e.

empty

half full

c.   f.

6. Count the number in each stack.

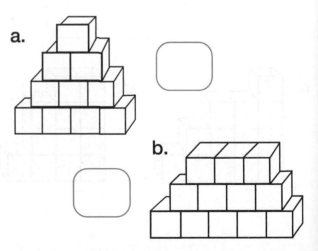

a.

b.

Volume and Capacity	Measuring Capacity

1. Colour the container that holds the **most**.

2. Number the containers 1 to 6 from **smallest** to **largest**.

3. Tick the can that could be **empty**.

4. Colour the container best used to fill a bucket.

5. Colour the numbers of cups or mugs full of water needed to fill a juice bottle.

6. About how many cups full of tea might you get from a tea pot? Colour a cup for each pour.

7. Colour the object that would hold the **most** amount of water. Tick the **least**.

Measuring Mass - Weight

Comparing and Ordering Mass

1. Colour the **heavy** objects.

2. Colour the **light** objects.

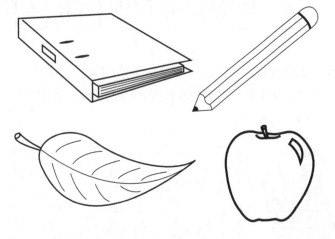

3. Tick the **heaviest** object.

4. Colour the **heavy** object.

a.

b.

c.
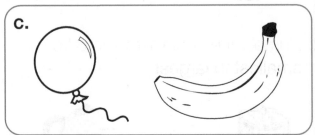

d.

5. Order the mass of these people 1 to 4.

New Syllabus Mentals and Extension K, Early Stage One

Mass and its Features

1. Colour the two that are about as **heavy** as each other.

2. Colour the ones easy to **roll**.

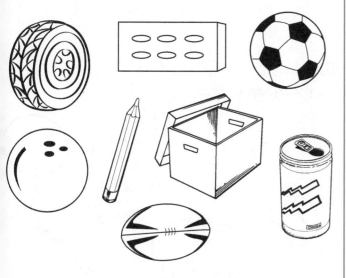

3. Draw two things **lighter** that the girl.

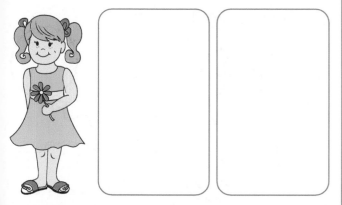

Comparing Mass

4. Colour the **heavy** one.

5. Colour the object that is **light** on the see saw.

a.

b.

6. Colour the see saw that **might** balance.

a.

b.

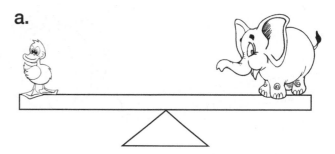

7. Draw two things heavier than an orange.

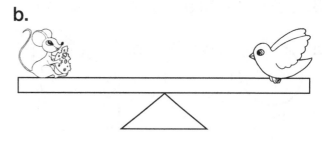

1. Colour the **light** objects.

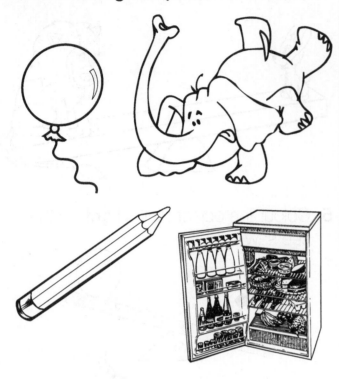

2. Colour the **light** objects.

3. Colour the **heavy** objects in each group.

a.

b.

c.

d.

4. Colour the **lightest** object in each group

a.
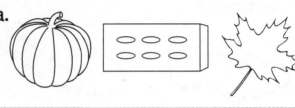

b.

5. Trace over the word light then colour the **light** objects

6. Trace over the word light then colour the **heavy** objects

7. Colour the **light** objects.

1. Tick and colour the logs that are the **same** lengths.

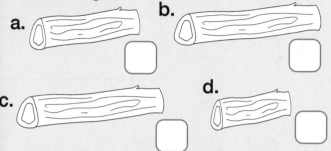

2. Tick and colour the object **longer** than a ruler.

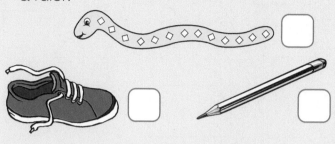

3. Which mat has a **larger** area? Colour it.

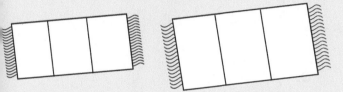

4. Order these areas 1-3 **smallest** to **largest**.

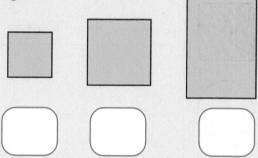

5. Which set of blocks has the **largest** volume? Colour it.

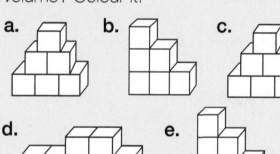

7. Colour the one that would hold the **most** water.

6. What is the total number of blocks in each of the others?

☐ each

9. Colour the number of cups full you might need to fill a kettle.

8. Tick the glass a **quarter** full.

10. Colour the things **lighter** than a brick.

11. Tick the beam balance that is **most likely** true.

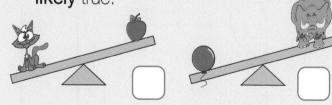

12. Colour the **light** things.

13. Trace over the word. *heavy*

1. Colour the triangles.

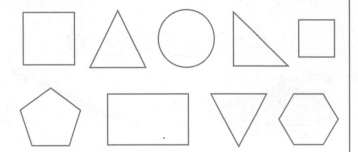

2. Name these shapes.

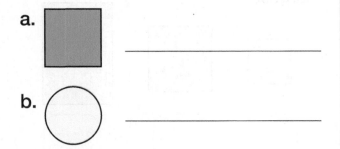

a. _____

b. _____

c. _____

3. How many sides on each shape?

a. square ⬜ **b.** triangle ⬜

c. pentagon ⬜ **d.** hexagon ⬜

e. circle ⬜ **f.** rectangle ⬜

4. Colour the rectangles.

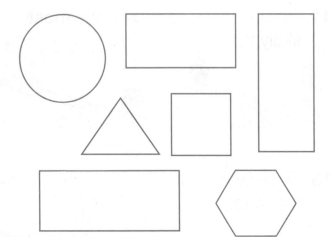

5. Trace around each shape then colour and name it.

a. 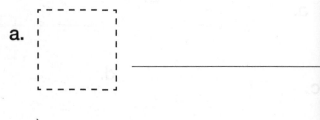 _____

b. 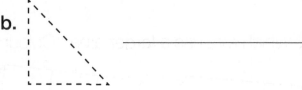 _____

c. 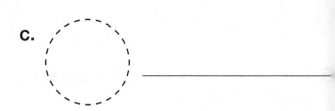 _____

6. Complete the features.

a. A square has ⬜ corners.

b. A circle has ⬜ corners.

c. A triangle has ⬜ corners.

d. A rectangle has ⬜ corners.

7. Name these shapes.

a.  _____

b.  _____

c.  _____

2D Shape and Features	2D Shapes

1. Colour the squares in this group.

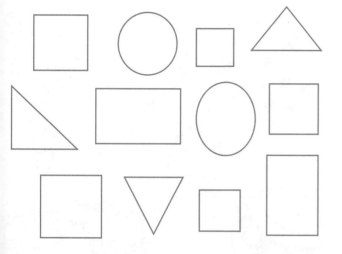

2. Colour the shapes with sloping or curved sides.

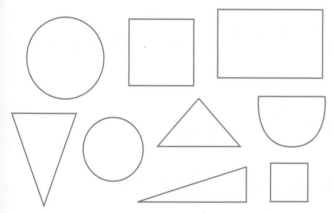

3. Match the square to the group it best belongs.

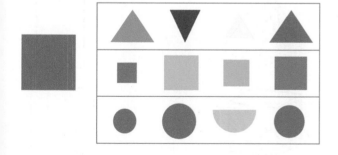

4. Write Yes or No to each sentence.

a. A square has 4 sides. _____

b. A triangle has
1 curved surface. _____

c. A rectangle has 4 corners. _____

d. A pentagon has 5 sides. _____

5. Draw these shapes in a box.

a. triangle

b. circle

c. square

6. Match the triangle to the group to it best belongs.

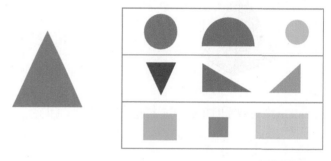

7. How many sides on a circle?

8. How many corners on a square?

9. How many corners on a pentagon?

10. How many curved lines on a rectangle?

11. Colour the rectangles blue and those with curved surfaces red.

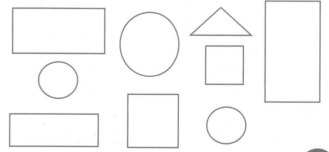

1. Match the 3D shape to its name.

a.

pyramid

b.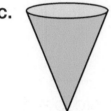

cube

c.

cone

d.

cylinder

2. Tick the number of faces on a cube.

3 ☐   4 ☐   5 ☐   6 ☐

3. A pyramid has 5 corners?

Yes ☐   No ☐

4. Colour the **pyramids**.

 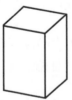

 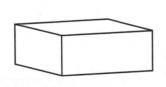

5. Colour the **spheres**.

6. Does the sphere have **sharp corners**?

Y ◯   N ◯

7. Can a sphere **roll** easily?   Y ◯   N ◯

8. Are spheres **round**?   Y ◯   N ◯

9. Match the **3D** object to a face.

New Syllabus Mentals and Extension K, Early Stage On

1. Draw a line from the object to its name.

a.

sphere

b.

pyramid

c.

cylinder

d.

cone

e.
ice block

cube

2. Colour all the **spheres**.

3. How many sides on a cube?

4. Colour the 3D object that will **roll**.

5. Colour the **prisms**.

6. Colour the **prisms**.

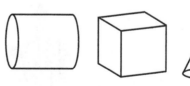

7. Colour the **cones**.

Sorting 3D Objects

1. Colour the shape that does **NOT** belong.

a.

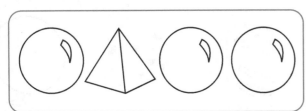

b.

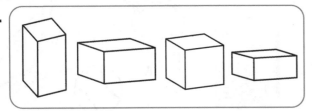

c.

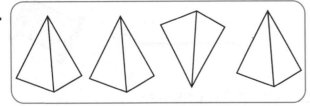

d.

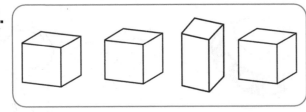

2. Draw a line from each object to its shadow.

a.

b.

c.

d.

Extension 2D Shapes and 3D Objects

1. Colour the **square** in this group.

2. How many sides and corners on a

SHAPE	SIDES	CORNERS
a. triangle		
b. square		
c. circle		

3. How many shapes have curved sides in this group?

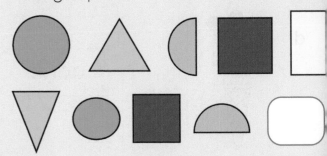

4. Colour the **cylinder**.

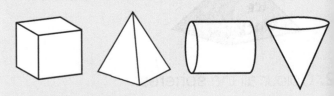

5. Name this object.

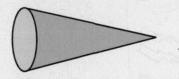
_____

6. How many faces on a cube?

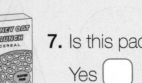

7. Is this packet a prism?

Yes ☐   No ☐

8. Is a balloon a sphere?

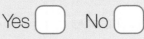

Yes ☐   No ☐

New Syllabus Mentals and Extension K, Early Stage On

1. Draw an orange in the **middle** of this group. Colour it orange.

2. Draw a straw for these cans.

a.

b.

c.

(along side) (above) (in front)

3. Match the soft drink to its label. The straw is:

(behind)

(on top of)

(inside)

4. Draw a pencil **above** and **below** this one.

5. Draw a bowl in **front** of the dog and a bone **behind** it.

6. Colour the things that are **upside down**.

7. Colour the pair that is **back to back**.

a. **b.**

8. Colour the **nearest** tree.

1. Draw 4 fish **inside** the bowl.

2. Draw a garbage bin and a letter box **in front** of the house.

3. Colour the **middle** one in each group.

a.

b.

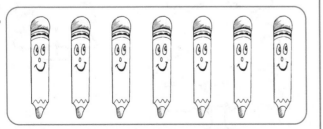

4. Draw an apple **along side** the fruit bowl on the **left**. and an orange on the **right**.

5. Tick the **right** foot.

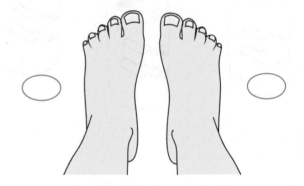

6. Colour the **left** hand and foot.

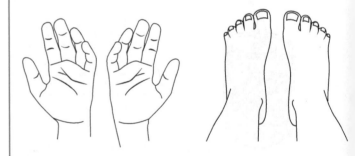

7. Draw a ball **behind** the boy.

8. Draw an arrow head pointing **right**.

1. Draw a **smaller** tree on the **right** of this one and a **taller** tree on the **left**.

2. Colour the building **further** away.

3. Draw a letter box in **front** of the **nearest** building.

4. Colour the arrows pointing **right**.

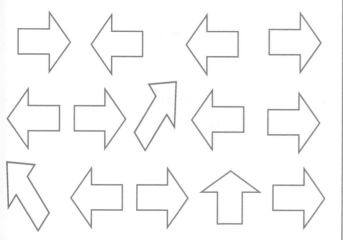

5. Colour the path to the **newsagents**.

NEWSAGENTS

SERVICE STATION

6. Did you pass the school?

Yes ◯   No ◯

7. Did you go to the park?

Yes ◯   No ◯

8. Did you cross the bridge?

Yes ◯   No ◯

9. Tick what is opposite the newsagents.

Bridge ◯   School ◯

Service Station ◯

10. Draw an arrow head pointing **left**.

Position and Direction

1. Follow the instructions below to plot a path home.

Start Here→					
					🏠

Move straight ahead 4 spaces

Move down 2 spaces

Go left 2 spaces

Go down one space

Go left 2 spaces

Go down 2 spaces

Go right 5 spaces to home

2. Number the runners from **1st** to **last**.

3.

a. Colour the pencil on the **far right** red.

b. Colour the **second** pencil blue.

c. Colour the **middle** pencil yellow.

Position - Extension

4. In what position is the chair? Colour the answer.

(right) (left) (middle)

5. What is on **top** of the table?

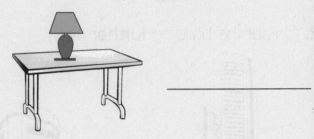

_____

6. Colour the arrows pointing **left**.

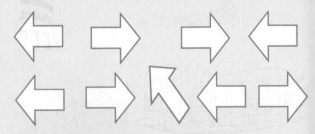

7. Colour the **middle** cupcake pink.

8. Draw a banana **in front** of the bowl and another orange to its **right**.

9. Draw a bat **in front** of the boy and a football **behind** him.

New Syllabus Mentals and Extension K, Early Stage On

Day and Night	**Morning/Afternoon**

1. Draw a line from the pictures showing 'day' or 'night'.

day

night

4. Join the words to the best picture.

morning   afternoon

5. Tick the **morning** pictures.

2. Tick the **daytime** pictures.

6. Colour the **afternoon** sun.

3. Colour the **night-time** picture.

7. Draw an **afternoon** picture.

Days of the Week

1. Add missing days of the week.

Sunday

_____

Tuesday

Wednesday

_____

_____

Saturday

2. How many days in **one week**? ⬜

3. What is the day **before** Friday?

_____

4. What is the day **after** Sunday?

_____

5. What days make up the weekend?

_____

_____

6. Name the **last** school day in a week.

_____

7. What is the **first** day of a school week.

_____

Know Your Days of the Week

8. Write the day after each of these.

a. **Wednesday** _____

b. **Saturday** _____

c. **Tuesday** _____

d. **Sunday** _____

9. Tick the **weekend** pictures.

10. Circle the day in the wrong order.

Monday

Tuesday

Wednesday

Friday

Thursday

11. How many days in a fortnight? ⬜

12. What day is the middle of the week? _____

   New Syllabus Mentals and Extension K, Early Stage One

Days of the Week

1. Write the day to match the order starting at Sunday.

6th _____

4th _____

3rd _____

1st _____

5th _____

7th _____

2nd _____

2. Write the day that comes **before** these days.

a. _____ Wednesday

b. _____ Saturday

c. _____ Tuesday

d. _____ Sunday

3. Tick Yes or No to answer these.

a. There are six school days in one week.

Yes ☐ No ☐

b. Half a fortnight is seven days

Yes ☐ No ☐

c. Tuesday comes after Monday in a week.

Yes ☐ No ☐

Long Time/Short Time

4. Tick the object that will take **longest** to fill.

5. Circle the one that takes the **longest** time to eat.

6. Colour the candle that will burn the **longest**.

a.   b.   c.

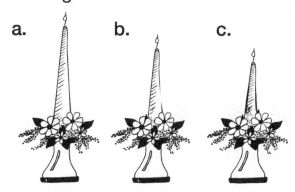

7. Colour the picture that would take the **longest** time to do.

Ordering Time Events

1. Order how these events happen from **1st** to **4th**.

a.

b.

c.

d.

2. Join the time words to the flowers.

a.

it began

b.

a few days later

c.
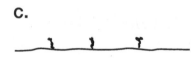

sometime later

d.

Look at them now

Events and Time

3. Order the events as they happen from 1-4.

a.

b.

c.

d.
 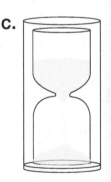

4. Colour the **slowest** to fill.

a. 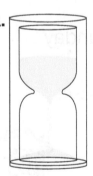 b. 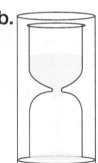 c.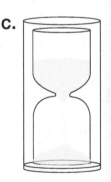

5. Write the order of the day's meals.

Lunch  Dinner

Breakfast

New Syllabus Mentals and Extension K, Early Stage On

Ordering Time

1. Colour the one born **second**.

2. Colour events that take a **short** time.

3. Order the days of the week where Sunday is 1st.

Tuesday ☐   Friday ☐

Wednesday ☐

Sunday [1st]   Monday ☐

Saturday ☐   Thursday ☐

Extension – Days, Weeks, Timing

1. Tick the **morning** picture.

☐   ☐   ☐

2. What days come **before** these.

a. _____ Tuesday

b. _____ Friday

3. A week has 7 days? Yes ☐ No ☐

4. Monday comes **before** Sunday?

Yes ☐   No ☐

5. The last day of the school week is Friday?   Yes ☐   No ☐

6. Colour the picture that would take the **longest** time to do.

7. Circle the one born **last**.

8. How many days in three weeks?

1. Write the time shown on the clocks.

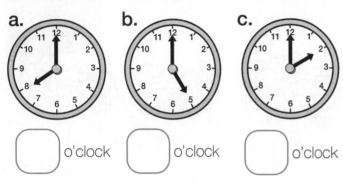

a. ☐ o'clock   b. ☐ o'clock   c. ☐ o'clock

2. Draw a little hand to show each time on the clock.

4 o'clock   7 o'clock   9 o'clock

3. Write the time shown on these clocks.

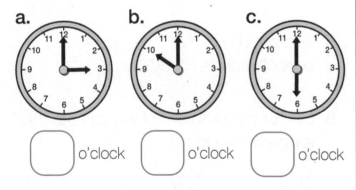

a. ☐ o'clock   b. ☐ o'clock   c. ☐ o'clock

4. Write the time shown on these clocks.

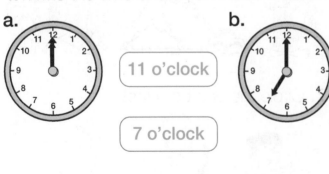

a.   b.   11 o'clock   7 o'clock

c.   12 o'clock   d.   4 o'clock

5. Draw a small hand on each clock to show the given time.

a. 3 o'clock   b. 7 o'clock   c. 2 o'clock

d. 10 o'clock   e. 4 o'clock   f. 9 o'clock

6. Draw a line from the activities to the time each could happen

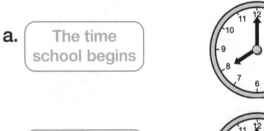

a. The time school begins

b. Time to have lunch

c. Time for school to finish

d. Time for breakfast

7. Write the time you go to bed.

_____

8. Draw hands on the clock to show 7 o'clock.

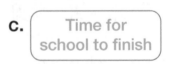

New Syllabus Mentals and Extension K, Early Stage One

Introducing Digital Time

1. Write the morning digital times on the digital clocks.

a. 7 o'clock

b. 5 o'clock

c. 3 o'clock

d. 10 o'clock

2. Write the morning digital time on the digital watches.

a. 11 o'clock

b. 2 o'clock

c. 8 o'clock

d. 12 o'clock

3. Write the o'clock time shown on each digital watch.

a.

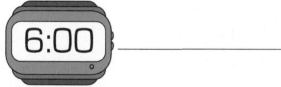 _____

b.

 _____

c.

 _____

Analogue and Digital Clocks

4. Write the morning as digital times.

a. 10 o'clock

b. 3 o'clock

5. Draw the digital time on the clock face .

a.

b.

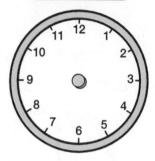

6. Draw a line the digital time to its correct clock face.

a.

b.

c.

7. Write the given time on the clock.

a.

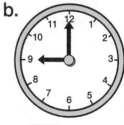

b.

 o'clock

o'clock

1. What time is shown on this clock?

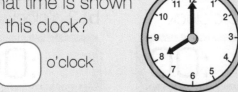

[ ] o'clock

2. Show the clock face time as digital time on the watch.

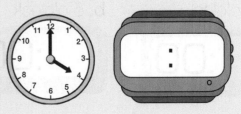

3. Add hands to the clock to show two o'clock.

4. Add the missing numbers to the clock.

5. Add hands to the clocks to show the hour time.

a. three o'clock   **b.** seven o'clock

6. Write the digital times on the clocks.

7. Show these times on the digital clocks.

a. twelve o'clock   **b.** one o'clock

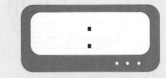 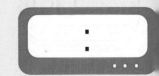

8. Write these times in words.

a. 8:00 _____

b. 2:00 _____

9. Add hands to the clocks to show these times.

a. four o'clock   **b.** ten o'clock

10. What time is shown on this clock?

_____

SWEET TREATS

From the graph:

1. Tick the sweet with **most**.

2. Tick the sweet with only **one**.

3. Tick the sweet with **less**.

4. Draw the sweet you would like to eat.

CUPCAKES AND FRUIT

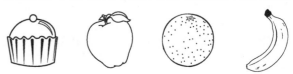

From the graph:

5. Colour the one with the **most** number

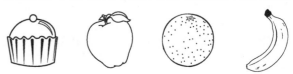

6. Colour the group with **4** objects

7. Colour the one that has the **less** number.

8. Colour the group with **3** objects.

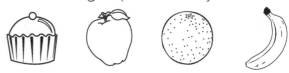

9. Colour the one you like to eat.

Shapes I Know

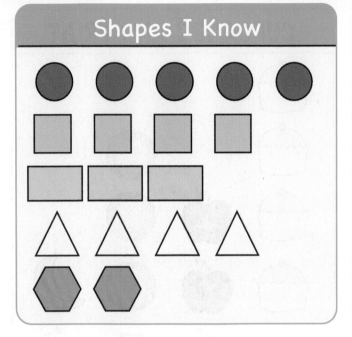

From the graph:

1. Tick the shape with **less**.

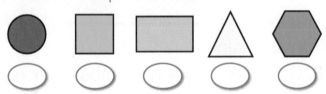

2. Tick the shapes with the **same** number in the graph.

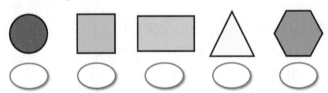

3. Tick the shape that has **3**.

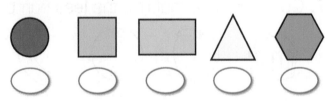

4. Tick the shape with the **most**.

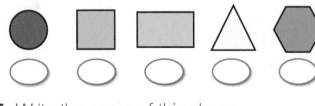

5. Write the name of this shape.

_____

Containers

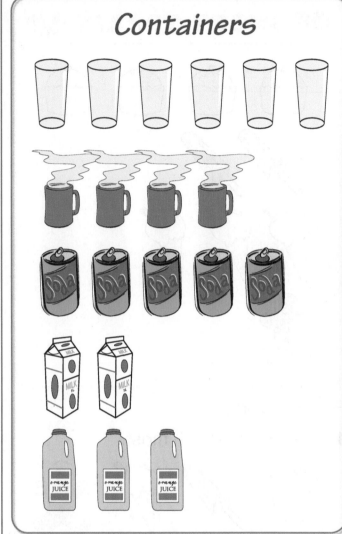

From the graph:

6. Colour the longest row

7. Is there the same number in each row?

Y ◯ N ◯

8. How many soft drinks are there? _____

9. Colour the row with less containers

10. Count the number of cups. _____

11. Are there more glasses than juice?

Y ◯ N ◯

12. Tick the container with only two.

13. How many containers in total? ◻

New Syllabus Mentals and Extension K, Early Stage On

Analysing List Graph

Fruits to Eat

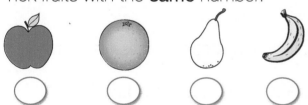

From the graph:

. Tick fruits with the **same** number.

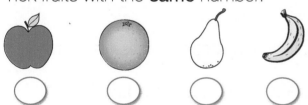

○   ○   ○   ○

. Colour the fruit with **most** pieces.

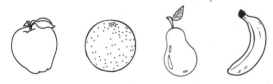

. Are there **more** pears than apples?

Yes ○   No ○

. There are 6 bananas? Yes ○ No ○

. Colour the fruit with **less** pieces.

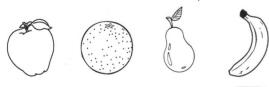

. How much fruit altogether? ▢

Reading a Picture Graph

Pets at the Pet Shop

From the graph:

7. The most popular pet is a bird?

Yes ▢   No ▢

8. Tick the pet which is the least popular.

9. How many more dogs are there than cats? ▢

10. How many more birds are there than frogs? ▢

11. How many pets in the pet shop? ▢

1. Sort these items into groups.

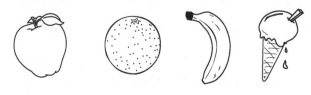

2. Colour which group has the **most**.

3. How many bananas?

4. How many ice creams?

5. Which group has the **least**? _____

Weather Chart

From the graph:

6. How many sunny days are there?

7. Are there three rainy days?

Yes   No

8. How many cloudy days are there?

9. How many more sunny days are there than rainy days?

10. Draw a picture of today's weather.

1. Colour the label that best describes the chance of an event happening.

2. Colour the chance card for these possible happenings.

a.

likely

unlikely

Rain tomorrow

a.

will happen

won't happen

might happen

b.

likely

unlikely

School tomorrow

b. will happen

won't happen

might happen

c.

likely

unlikely

Mow lawn today

c.

will happen

won't happen

might happen

d.

likely

unlikely

Sunny day tomorrow

d. will happen

won't happen

might happen

e.

likely

unlikely

Swimming tomorrow

e.

will happen

won't happen

might happen

f. will happen

won't happen

might happens

1.  and make [ ]

2.  take away leaves [ ]

3. Fill in the addition sentence.

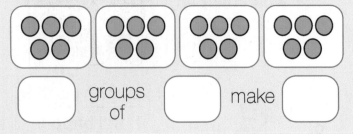

[ ] and [ ] make [ ]

4. Write the numbers in words.

a. 75 _____

b. 230 _____

5. Write how many in each group then complete the number sentence.

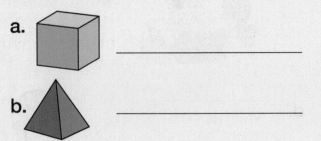

[ ] groups of [ ] make [ ]

6. Name these shapes.

a. 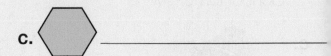 _____

b. _____

c. _____

7. Name these solid objects.

a. 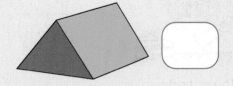 _____

b. _____

8. How many corners on this 3D objects.

 [ ]

9. What am I?
I am

I am round with five kangaroos on one face. I am gold in colour.

_____

10. How many $5 notes to make one hundred dollars? [ ]

11. Colour a quarter of this shape.

12. Colour the arrow pointing left.

13. What is the 5th letter of the alphabet? [ ]

14. Write the day before Monday.

_____

15. How many days in a fortnight? [ ]

16. Write the time shown on the clock.

_____

17. Write this time in words.

_____

Answers

p4
1. 1 2. ●━━➤ 3. one 4. dog, elephant 5. 1 6. 2
7. teacher 8. two 9. apples, spiders 10. 2

p5
1. 3 3 3 3 2. teacher 3. three 4. balloons
5. 3 apples 6. 1-one, 2-two, 3-three 7.a. 3 b. 3
c. 2 8. one 9. 2

p6
1. 4 4 4 4 2. 3. four
4. ginger bread men/ cupcakes 5.a. 3 b. 4
6.a. 4 b. 4 c. 4 7. 4-four, 2-two, 3-three, 1-one
8. 2 9. 1

p7
1. 5 5 5 5 2. teacher 3. five, five 4. 2_4,5
5. 5 balloons 6.a. 3 b. 4 c. 2 7. 4_2,1
8. 9.a. 5 b. 5 10. 4/2

p8
1. 6 6 6 6 2. teacher 3.a. 4 b. 5 c. 6 d. 4
4. six, six 5.a. 4 b. 3 6. 7.a. 6 b. 6 8. 6/6
9. 2_5,6 10. 2 more

p9
1. seven 7, seven 7 2. Colour 7 leaves 2 3. 4,5_7
4.a. 2 b. 5 c. 3 5.a. 6 b. 7 6. 7 dots, 7 dots,
7 dots 7.a. 4 b. 2 8.a. 2 b. 4 9.a. 5 fish
b. 7 fish 10. 6,5_3_1

p10
1. 8 8 8 8 2. teacher 3.b. 8 stars 4.a. 5_7 b. 3_5
c. 6_8 d. 4_6 5. eight eight 6.a. 9 dots b. 8 dots
c. 8 dots 7. 3 and 5 make 8 fish 8. 4 9.a. 4 b. 5
10.a. 8 b. 2

p11
1. 9 9 9 9 9 2. teacher 3.a. 5 dots b. 4 dots
c. 3 dots d. 6 dots 4. 5_7_9 5. nine, nine
6. 9 eggs 7.a. 8 b. 7 c. 6 d. 5 e. 4 8.a. 4 b. 8
c. 2 9.a. 9 b. 4 10.a. 5 b. 6 c. 4

p12
1. 10 10 10 10 2.b. 10 counters 3. teacher
4.a. 6 b. 2 c. 5 5.a. b. c.
6. ten, ten, ten 7.a. 10 b. 2 c. 7 d. 6 e. 5
8.a. 7 b. 5 9.a. 8 b. 3 10.a. 4 b. 7 11.a. 5 b. 2

p13
1. 0 0 0 0 2. bowl 3. zero, zero 4. 0,1,2,3,4,5
5.a. 3/0 b. 6/0 6. 7.
8.a. 0 b. 0 c. 0
9.a. 0 b. 0
10.a. 0 b. 0 c. 0

p14
Extension 1.a. eight b. nine c. two d. six e. four
f. seven g. zero h. one i. five j. three k. ten
2. 9,8,7_5 3.a. 7,8 b. 6,7 c. 9,10 4.a. 4/6 b. 5/8
c. 7/8 5. (6) (4) 6.a. 7 b. 8

p15
1. 1st-first, 5th-fifth, 7th-seventh, 10th-tenth
2.
3. 2nd, 3rd,_ _ 6th 4. 5. teacher
6. 'd' 7. 8th
8. 9. first-1st, third-3rd, sixth-6th,
   second-2nd
[4th] [3rd] [2nd] [1st] 10.a. 1st, 2nd, 3rd
b. 7th,8th,9th c. 5th,6th,7th 11. letter 'g'

p16
1. 11 eleven b. 12 twelve c. 13 thirteen
2. group b (12 balls) 3.a. 10_12 b. 9_11 c. 11_13
d. 8_10 4.a. 11,12,13 b. 11,10,9 5.a. 12 stars
b. 13 apples 6.a. 12 dots b. 11 dots 7. 13 fish
8.a. 8 b. 2 9.a. 11 b. 13 c. 12

p17
1.a. fourteen-14, 14 b. fifteen-15,15
c. sixteen-16, 16 2.a. 15 b. 14 c. 16 3.a. 4 b. 11
4. 12,13_ _ 16 5.a. 14_16 b. 11_13 c. 13_15
d. 12_14 6. teacher 7.a. 13 b. 16 c. 14 d. 16
8.a. 6 b. 5 9. 16,15,13 10. 16 triangles

p18
1.a. 17, 17, seventeen b. 18, 18, eighteen
2.a. 17 apples b. 16 3.a. 16_18 b. 17_19
4.a. 12,13,15,16 b. 17,16_14_12 5.a. 18 b. 17
6. 19,19,20,20 7.c. apples 8.a. 12 b. 5
9. 19 take away 5 =14 10. 13,14,15,16,17,18,19

p19
Extension - Review 1.a. 6_8 b. 11_13 2. 20 dots
3. eight 8 , twelve 12, six 6, zero 0, fourteen 14,
nine 9, seventeen 17, twelve 12 4.a. 17 b. 14
c. 20 d. 16 5. 3,4,6,9,10,12,13,15,16,18,20
6. 6 dots 7.a. 15 b. 18 8. 20,19,18,17,16,15,14
9. 15 take away 5 leaves 10 pegs 10.a. 13 b. 17
c. 19 11. letter 'f' 12. twenty

p20
1. teacher (2x5) 2.a. 2 and 4 make 6 b. 3 and 3
make 6 c. 3 and 2 make 5 3.a. 5 b. 4 c. 6
4.a. 13 b. 12 c. 17 5. teacher (3x3) 6.a. 8 b. 6
c. 4 7. 8.a. 6 b. 7 c. 5
9.a.14 stars b. 12 counters

p21
1.a. 1 b. 9 c. 7 2.a. 3 and 5 make 8
b. 5 and 4 make 9 c. 5 and 5 make 10
3.a. 3 and 7 make 10 b. 4 and 6 and 5 make 15
4.a. 7 b. 8 5.a. 6 b. 5 c. 3 6. teacher (4)+(2) - 5
and 5 make 10 7.a. 5 and 5 make 10
b. 3 and 5 make 8

p22
1.a. 5 b. 11 c. 9 2.a. 13 b. 15 c. 9
3.a. 6 and 4 and 8 make 18
b. 7 and 3 and 6 make 16 4.a. 16 b. 18
5.a. 3 and 4 and 2 make 9
  b. 5 and 1 and 3 make 9 6.a. 5 b. 5 c. 3
7.a. 12 b. 13 c. 13 8. 5 and 6 and 6 make 17

p23
1.a. 9 2.a. 4 and 3 make 7
b. 4 and 6 make 10
b. 7 c. 6 and 2 make 8
3.a. 8 4.a. 7 and 5 make 12
b.9 and 5 make 14
b. 6 c.5 and 8 make 13
5.a. 6 and 5 and 3 make 14
  b. 4 and 5 and 4 make 13 6.a. 13 b. 13

p24
1.a. ○ b. ■ c. ▲ 2. 3.
4. 5. 6. 7.
8.

Answers

p25
Extension 1. 15 2. 5 and 7 make 12 3. 15 stars
4. 8 and 7 make 15 cakes 5.a. 8 b. 7
6. 8 and 4 and 3 make 15 7. 6 and 9 make 15
8. 8 and 4 make 12
9.a. 12 b. 17 c. 18 10. 19 matches
11. 6 and 5 and 2 make 13 12.
13. 20

p26
1.a. 10 take away 4 leaves 6
   b. 11 take away 5 leaves 6
   c. 10 take away 6 leaves 4
   d. 8 take away 3 leaves 5
   e. 14 take away 5 leaves 9
2.a. 9 take away 3 leaves 6
   b. 13 take away 8 leaves 5
   c. 10 take away 3 leaves 7
3.a. 3 b. 5 4.a. 3 b. 7 c. 2

p27
1. 7 take away 4 leaves 3
2. 13 take away 8 leaves 5 3.a. 3 b. 4
4.a. 5 b. 6 c. 5 d. 2 5.a. 6 b. 8 c. 8 d. 6
6.a. 11 take away 7 leaves 4
   b. 9 take away 4 leaves 5
7. teacher - 15 take away leaves 6 8. 3

p28
1.a. 9 take away 7 leaves 2
   b. 12 take away 7 leaves 5
2.a. 10 take away 5 leaves 5 b. 8 take away 6 leaves 2
3.a. 14 take away 7 leaves 7
   b. 12 take away 9 leaves 3
4.a. 8 take away 6 leaves 2 b. 9 take away 5 leaves 4
5.a. 10 take away 2 leaves 8
   b. 7 take away 4 leaves 3
   c. 9 take away 7 leaves 2
6.a. 4 b. 5 c. 6

p29
1.a. 4 small circles 2.a. ○ b. △ c. ▲ 3. cupcake
4. △ 5. cat -animals, apple - fruit, fish - sea creatures
6. line a. ● b. □ and △ 7.a. left hand
b. cupcake c. mouse

p30
1. table, elephant, chair 2. apples, pears, coconut
3. 4. plane, butterfly, kite 5. 5 and 5
6. 2 groups of 5 balls make 10 7. teacher
8. 2 groups of 4 stars make 8
9.a. 3 groups of 4 make 12 b. 4 groups of 3 make 8

p31
1. 3 groups of 3 make 9 2. colour 2x5
3. 2 groups of 5 make 10 4. add 4 fish
5. 4 different colours of 4 counters, 4 x 4 =16
6.a. b. 7.a. 2 groups
   of 5 make 10
b. 4 groups of 2 make 8 8.
9. 3 groups of 5 make 15

p32
Extension 1. 10 take away 3 leaves 7
2. 9 take away 5 leaves 4 3.a. 3 b. 6 c. 7 d. 9
4. 15 take away 7 leaves 8 5.a. 9 b. 12 c. 3 d. 8
6.a. 18 take away 11 leaves 7
b. 19 take away 16 leaves 3 7. ☐ 8. 22 9. cat
10.a. 3 groups of 2 make 6 b. 2 groups of 3 make 6
11. 4 groups of 3 make 12 12.

p33
1. 2. ten cents five cents
twenty cents fifty cents
one dollar two dollars
3. 5 4. 10 cents 5. 5c, 10c, 20c,
50c, $1, $2 6.a. 80c b. $1.55
7.a. $2 cupcake b. 50c apple
c. 20c lolly

p34
1. $1.35 2. 50c+20c+10c 3.a. 85c b. $3.60
c. $4.50 4.a. $2+$1+50c+20c b. $2+20c+20c
c. $1+50c+20c+5c 5.a. five dollars b. fifty dollars
c. twenty dollars d. one hundred dollars e. ten dollars
6.a. $50 b. $20 c. $10 d. $5 e. $100
7. $5, $10, $20, $50, $100 8. $5 9. 4

p35
1. ten dollars 2.a. $50 - helmet b. $5 - chips
c. $100 - cricket bat 3.a. apple - 50 cents
b. cake - $2 c. bananas - 50 cents 4.a. $10.10
b. $15.20 5.a. blue b. red c. green 6.a. $1+20c
b. $2+50c+5c c. all 20c coins 7.
8. icecream, bread, shoes
9. 5x$10 10. $81.70

p36
1. 2.
3.
4.a. 5.a. b. c. d.
6.a. 3 oranges b. 2 mice c. 5 balloons
7.a. 6 b. 4 c. 10 d. 5 8. 12 half apples

p37
1. any one quarter
2.
3.a. b. c. 4. teacher 5.
6.a. 2 apples b. 3 fish c. 4 balls
7.a. quarter b. half c. half d. quarter e. half f. half
g. quarter 8.a. 5 b. 25 c. 9 d. 2

p38
1. zig zag, curved,
straight, dotted 2. a,b,e
3.a. b. c. d. 4.a. b. c.
5. teacher
Extension 1. twenty cents 2. 50 cents 3. $3.60
4.a. pink b. yellow 5. 50c+20c+10c 6. 10x$10
7. No 8. 1/2 9. 10. 3 balls
11. one square

New Syllabus Mentals and Extension K, Early Stage On

Answers

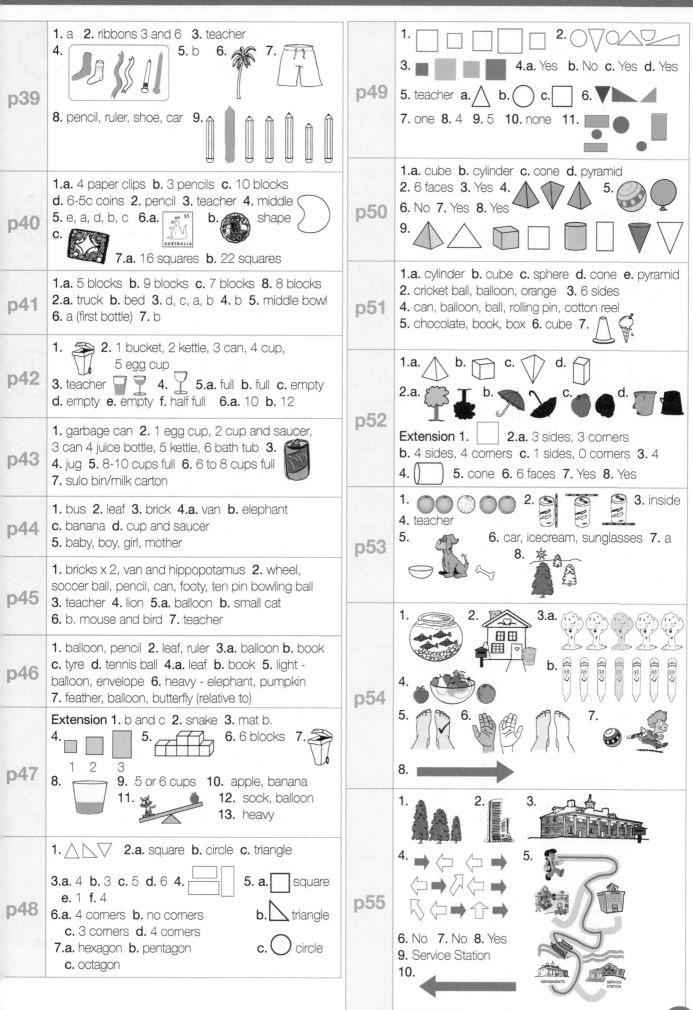

p39
1. a 2. ribbons 3 and 6 3. teacher
4. [images of sock, ribbon, pencil, crayon]
5. b 6. [palm tree] 7. [shorts]
8. pencil, ruler, shoe, car 9. [pencils]

p40
1.a. 4 paper clips b. 3 pencils c. 10 blocks
d. 6-5c coins 2. pencil 3. teacher 4. middle
5. e, a, d, b, c 6.a. [stamp] b. [coin] shape
c. [tile]
7.a. 16 squares b. 22 squares

p41
1.a. 5 blocks b. 9 blocks c. 7 blocks 8. 8 blocks
2.a. truck b. bed 3. d, c, a, b 4. b 5. middle bowl
6. a (first bottle) 7. b

p42
1. [bin] 2. 1 bucket, 2 kettle, 3 can, 4 cup,
5 egg cup
3. teacher [cup][glass] 4. [glass] 5.a. full b. full c. empty
d. empty e. empty f. half full 6.a. 10 b. 12

p43
1. garbage can 2. 1 egg cup, 2 cup and saucer,
3 can 4 juice bottle, 5 kettle, 6 bath tub 3. [can]
4. jug 5. 8-10 cups full 6. 6 to 8 cups full
7. sulo bin/milk carton

p44
1. bus 2. leaf 3. brick 4.a. van b. elephant
c. banana d. cup and saucer
5. baby, boy, girl, mother

p45
1. bricks x 2, van and hippopotamus 2. wheel,
soccer ball, pencil, can, footy, ten pin bowling ball
3. teacher 4. lion 5.a. balloon b. small cat
6. b. mouse and bird 7. teacher

p46
1. balloon, pencil 2. leaf, ruler 3.a. balloon b. book
c. tyre d. tennis ball 4.a. leaf b. book 5. light -
balloon, envelope 6. heavy - elephant, pumpkin
7. feather, balloon, butterfly (relative to)

p47
Extension 1. b and c 2. snake 3. mat b.
4. [squares 1 2 3] 5. [blocks] 6. 6 blocks 7. [bin]
8. [cup] 9. 5 or 6 cups 10. apple, banana
11. [seesaw] 12. sock, balloon
13. heavy

p48
1. [triangles] 2.a. square b. circle c. triangle
3.a. 4 b. 3 c. 5 d. 6 4. [rectangles] 5. a. [square] square
e. 1 f. 4
6.a. 4 corners b. no corners b. [triangle] triangle
c. 3 corners d. 4 corners
7.a. hexagon b. pentagon c. [circle] circle
c. octagon

p49
1. [squares] 2. [shapes]
3. [squares] 4.a. Yes b. No c. Yes d. Yes
5. teacher a. [triangle] b. [circle] c. [square] 6. [triangles]
7. one 8. 4 9. 5 10. none 11. [shapes]

p50
1.a. cube b. cylinder c. cone d. pyramid
2. 6 faces 3. Yes 4. [triangles] 5. [ball, balloon]
6. No 7. Yes 8. Yes
9. [pyramid, triangle, cube, square, cylinder, triangles]

p51
1.a. cylinder b. cube c. sphere d. cone e. pyramid
2. cricket ball, balloon, orange 3. 6 sides
4. can, balloon, ball, rolling pin, cotton reel
5. chocolate, book, box 6. cube 7. [cone, icecream]

p52
1.a. [pyramid] b. [cube] c. [kite] d. [box]
2.a. [tree] b. [umbrella] c. [olives] d. [bucket]
Extension 1. [square] 2.a. 3 sides, 3 corners
b. 4 sides, 4 corners c. 1 sides, 0 corners 3. 4
4. [cylinder] 5. cone 6. 6 faces 7. Yes 8. Yes

p53
1. [oranges] 2. [cans] 3. inside
4. teacher
5. [dog, bowl, bone] 6. car, icecream, sunglasses 7. a
8. [sun, trees]

p54
1. [fishbowl] 2. [house] 3.a. [trees]
b. [pencils]
4. [fruit bowl]
5. [feet] 6. [hands] 7. [child running]
8. [arrow]

p55
1. [trees] 2. [building] 3. [building]
4. [arrows] 5. [map]
6. No 7. No 8. Yes
9. Service Station
10. [arrow]

Answers

p56
1. Start Here X X X X (grid with X's marked)
2. (figures running) 4th 3rd 2nd 1st
3. (pencils)
4. middle
5. light/lamp
6. (arrows)
7. (cupcakes)
8. (fruit bowl)
9. (rugby ball, running figure, cricket bat)

p57
1. day - sandwich, mowing, sun shining night - bed
2. swimming, classroom 3. watching TV, sleeping
4. wake up/ sun down 5. cleaning teeth/ going to
school 6. colour first picture of the sun 7. teacher

p58
1. Monday, Thursday, Friday 2. 7 days 3. Thursday
4. Monday 5. Saturday, Sunday 6. Friday
7. Monday 8.a. Thursday b. Sunday c. Wednesday
d. Monday 9. netball, soccer, swimming 10. Friday
11. 14 days 12. Wednesday

p59
1. 6th - Friday, 4th - Wednesday, 3rd - Tuesday, 1st
Sunday, 5th Thursday, 7th Saturday, 2nd Monday
2.a. Tuesday b. Friday c. Monday d. Saturday
3.a. No b. Yes c. Yes 4. bath tub 5. watermelon
6. a. 7. sleeping in bed

p60
1. 1st 'b', 2nd 'd', 3rd 'a', 4th 'c'
2. 'c' - it began, 'd' - a few days later,
   'a' - sometime later, 'b' - look at them now
3. 'c' - first, 'a' - second, 'b'-third, 'd'-fourth
4. 'b' slowest (narrow opening)
5. 1 - breakfast, 2 - lunch, 3 - dinner

p61
1. teenage girl 2. clean your teeth 3. 1st Sunday,
2nd Monday, 3rd Tuesday, 4th Wednesday, 5th
Thursday, 6th Friday, 7th Saturday
Extension 1. cleaning teeth 2.a. Monday
b. Thursday 3. Yes 4. No 5. Yes 6. mow the lawn
7. baby 8. 21 days

p62
1.a. 8 o'clock b. 5 o'clock c. 2 o'clock
2.a. (clock) b. (clock) c. (clock)
3.a. 3 o'clock b. 10 o'clock c. 6 o'clock
4.a. 12 o'clock b. 7 o'clock c. 4 o'clock d. 11o' clock
5.a. (clock) b. (clock) c. (clock)
d. (clock) e. (clock) f. (clock)

p62
6.a. (clock) b. (clock) c. (clock) d. (clock)
7. teacher 8. (clock)

p63
1.a. 7:00 b. 5:00 c. 3:00 d. 10:00
2.a. 11:00 b. 2:00 c. 8:00 d. 12:00
3.a. six o'clock b. four o'clock c. one o'clock
4.a. 10:00 b. 3:00 5.a. (clock) b. (clock)
6.a. 1:00 b. 10:00 c. 6:00 7.a. 5 o'clock
(clocks) b. 9 o'clock

p64
Extension 1. 8 o'clock 2. 4:00
3. (clock) 4. (clock) 5.a. (clock) b. (clock)
6.a. 8:00 b. 5:00 7.a. 12:00 b. 1:00
8.a. 8 o'clock b. 2 o'clock
9.a. (clock) b. (clock) 10. three o'clock

p65
1. cupcake 2. gingerbread man 3. gingerbread man
4. teacher 5. cupcakes 6. oranges 7. bananas
8. apples 9. teacher

p66
1. hexagon 2. squares and triangles 3. rectangles
4. circles 5. triangle 6. glasses 7. No 8. 5 cans
9. milk 10. 4 cups 11. Yes 12. milk 13. 20

p67
1. apples and bananas 2. pears 3. Yes
4. No 5 bananas 5. oranges 6. 18 pieces
7. No - dog 8. fish 9. 2 10. 2 11. 20 pets

p68
1. apples - 3, oranges - 6, bananas - 4,
icecream cones - 4 2. oranges 3. 4 bananas
4. 4 icecreams 5. apples 6. 5 sunny days 7. Yes
8. 4+3 rainy 9. 2 more 10. teacher

p69
1.a. unlikely b. likely c. unlikely d. likely e. unlikely
2.a. won't happen b. will happen c. might happen
d. will happen e. won't happen f. won't happen

p70
Final Extension 1. 11 2. 9 3. 4 and 11 make 15
4.a. seventy-five b. two hundred and thirty
5. 4 groups of 5 make 20
6.a. square b. triangle c. hexagon
7.a. cube b. pyramid 8. 6 9. one dollar 10. 20
11. (triangle) any one only triangle 12. (arrow)
13. letter 'e' 14. Sunday 15. 14 16. 7 o'clock
17. three o'clock

New Syllabus Mentals and Extension K, Early Stage On